AFRICAN AMERICANS
and the
LOCAL CHURCH

Edited by ROBERT H. KING

SAINT LOUIS

Scripture quotations, unless otherwise indicated, are from the King James or Authorized Version of the Bible.

Verses marked NIV are taken from the HOLY BIBLE, NEW INTERNATIONAL VERSION®. NIV®. Copyright © 1973, 1978, 1984 by International Bible Society. Used by permission of Zondervan Publishing House. All rights reserved.

Scripture quotations marked RSV are from the Revised Standard Version of the Bible, copyrighted 1946, 1952, © 1971, 1973 by the Division of Christian Education of the National Council of the Churches of Christ in the U.S.A., and are used by permission.

Copyright © 1996 Concordia Publishing House
3558 S. Jefferson Avenue, St. Louis, MO 63118-3968
Manufactured in the United States of America

Library of Congress Cataloging-in-Publication Data.

African Americans and the local church/edited by Robert H. King.
    Includes bibliographical references.
    ISBN 0-570-04862-1
    1. Afro-American Lutherans. 2. Church work with Afro-Americans.
3. Lutheran Church—Missouri Synod—Membership. 4. Lutheran Church—
United States—Membership.   I. King, Robert H., 1922-
BX8060.N5A35   1996
284.1'322'08996073—dc20   96-5131
                                             CIP

1 2 3 4 5 6 7 8 9 10   05 04 03 02 01 00 99 98 97 96

Contents

Acknowledgments   5

Preface   7

Contributors   9

1 **Historical Reflections of African Americans and
    Parochial Schools**   13
  ROBERT H. KING

2 **Urban Ministry, the Church's Inescapable Challenge**   31
  RICHARD C. DICKINSON

3 **Worship in the African American Church**   50
  WILLIAM H. GRIFFEN

4 **Ministry in a Multiethnic Parish**   72
  KERMIT H. RATCLIFFE

5 **Church Work in Rural Communities**   93
  ROBERT H. KING

6 **African American Families and the Church**   110
  PHILLIP A. CAMPBELL

7 **The Future of Black Ministry in the Church**   122
  BRYANT E. CLANCY, JR.

Appendix A Favorite Negro Spirituals   142

Appendix B Some Pioneers of Lutheranism among Blacks   151

Appendix C Clergy Roster   154

Acknowledgments

Sincere words cannot adequately express the depth of my gratitude to those who have helped immeasurably in the preparation of this anthology. I offer commendations to the faithful contributing authors associated with me in writing the book's contents—for their tolerance, patience, understanding, and skills under my persistent prompting to meet a creditable deadline. My heart cannot hold enough thanks to Dr. Jean King, my faithful wife and a member of the graduate faculty at Drury College, for her tireless, efficient assistance in editing the diversity of materials.

Mrs. Corinna Harton is praiseworthy beyond any words or phrases that I can muster to express appreciation for her sacrificial and patient secretarial work in bringing this task to its final stage. My mind and tongue cannot make known my overwhelming gratitude to Dr. August Suelflow, Retired Director of Concordia Historical Institute, for his wise counsel and unfailing encouragement in motivating me to pursue and complete this literary undertaking to the glory of God. I pray that this volume will result in more overt inclusiveness of all the redeemed people of Christ in His church.

Preface

The purpose of this anthology is to present major church situations faced by African Americans in the Lutheran church and society generally. Concerns are identified with which African Americans have been and still are affected as the redeemed people of God. Some noteworthy situations, concerns, experiences, problems, needs, and challenges encountered by African Americans are pointed out by the writers. Moreover, they disclose some of the cultures, lifestyles, mores, characteristics, customs, values, and traditions with which many African Americans are identified and in which they find meaning, purpose, and satisfying fulfillment as human beings created by the heavenly Father, redeemed by Jesus Christ, and called to be saints by the Holy Spirit.

This short volume's uniqueness lies in the fact that this is the first time six African American Lutheran pastors have collaboratively written a book. It is intended to be neither a panacea to cover all appearances of threatening despair nor a citadel of triumphant hope for African American Lutheran church people. Each writer addresses himself to a problematic topic or subject regarding African American Lutherans in certain locales and/or in diverse geographic areas, and endeavors to give some positive directives toward more meaningful, purposeful, and productive Christian lives according to each writer's own personal, theological, pastoral, social, and experiential insights. All the contributors to this book are ordained Lutheran ministers with tenures ranging from 23 to 45 years for a combined total of 204 years of ministerial service. The writers have served in urban and rural parishes in various sectors of the United States; in addition some of them hold or have held offices and positions at circuit, district, and synodical levels. Hence, the book's authors are recognized and respected for their abilities and services throughout the synodical church body.

Robert H. King, editor
Jefferson City, Missouri

Contributors

Phillip A. Campbell, Executive Director of Mission Networking, The Lutheran Church—Missouri Synod. For over 20 years he has served in urban parishes as pastor and counselor and occasionally as a college guest instructor. A 1971 graduate of Concordia Seminary, St. Louis, he holds a D.Min. degree from Howard University, Washington, D. C.

Bryant E. Clancy, Jr., Executive Director of the Board on Black Ministry, The Lutheran Church—Missouri Synod. He has served urban congregations, was executive director of urban ministries in Synod's Southeastern District, and has made recent exploratory visits to the Lutheran churches of Nigeria and Ghana. A 1961 graduate of Immanuel Lutheran Seminary, Greensboro, North Carolina, he received a D.Min. degree from McCormick Theological Seminary, Chicago.

Richard C. Dickinson, retired Executive Director of the Commission on Black Ministry, The Lutheran Church—Missouri Synod. He has served several rural and urban parishes, was guest instructor at Concordia College, Selma, Alabama, and has made two exploratory visits to the Lutheran Church of Nigeria, Africa. A 1952 graduate of Immanuel Lutheran Seminary, Greensboro, he received a D.Min. degree from Chicago Theological Seminary.

William H. Griffen, retired pastor of Zion Lutheran Church, Chicago, is instructor of theology at Lutheran High South, Chicago, and consultant for Wheat Ridge Foundation, Chicago, and for the Northern Illinois District of The Lutheran Church—Missouri Synod. He has served both rural and urban congregations. A 1951 graduate of Immanuel Lutheran Seminary, he was the recipient of a D.D. degree, Concordia Seminary, St. Louis.

Robert H. King, Second Vice-President of The Lutheran Church—Missouri Synod and pastor of Pilgrim Lutheran Church, Freedom, Missouri. He has served with rural and urban parishes and faculties at church and state institutions of higher education. He has made good-will trips to Canada, Mexico, Europe, and Africa. A 1949 graduate of Immanuel Lutheran Seminary, he received his Ph.D. degree from Indiana University, Bloomington, Indiana.

Kermit H. Ratcliffe, Associate Professor of Theology and Minority Director, Concordia University, Mequon, Wisconsin. His parishes have been in urban areas, and he has had noteworthy experience in multiethnic situations. A 1966 graduate of Concordia Theological Seminary, Springfield, Illinois, he received the S.T.M. degree from Concordia Seminary, St. Louis.

1

Historical Reflections of African Americans and Parochial Schools

Robert H. King

The purpose of this chapter is to reflect on the role of Lutheran parochial schools in rescuing African American children from the shackles of educational deficiencies. Moreover, it will disclose how these schools nurtured the minds of black children to educational accomplishments and spiritual enlightenment for more productive lives as children of God and as useful citizens of the American society. With a focus on the educational situation in the deep south where the writer was born and reared, much of this presentation will have a personal, experiential orientation.

During the first part of this century, a large number of African American children attended church-related elementary and secondary schools in specific areas of the south. Why? Were there no public schools? If so, why didn't they attend the public schools? Were the public schools inferior to church-related or parochial schools? Were church-related schools imposed or forced upon the children? Did the children attend the parochial schools as a matter of choice, or was it because of necessity? Were these schools free, as the public schools were? Did African Americans attend parochial schools because they were superior and of better quality than public schools?

A PROBLEMATIC CONCERN

The preceding questions are all important, and answers to them could be very extensive and enlightening. However, a chief reason African Americans went to church-related schools was because public schools in many areas of the south were available for white children only.

Of major importance for one to know is that education has been of lofty concern ever since African Americans arrived on American shores. For a majority of Americans, education was considered a chief means to upward mobility in social and economic opportunities. To shut off African Americans to educational systems was to uphold privileges of the white majority. Hence, the blacks' opportunities for upward mobility for upper economic opportunities were annihilated because of inherent educational deficiencies.

During slavery days, access to education for African Americans was rare. Some believe that blacks received no formal education in colonial America until the 18th century. Informal education was only slightly more available because many slave holders were against slaves learning to read. The pursuit of an adequate education has been a long, agonizing struggle for blacks. Some free blacks received limited instruction from free schools established by religious groups during the 18th and 19th centuries. However, as southern jim crowism became harsher, education of blacks became increasingly curtailed.

During the 1890s and early 1900s, the schools attended by African Americans were church-related and heavily supported by dedicated church people. Examples of some of these schools as identified in Alabama:

Schools	Counties	Supporting Churches
Baggot	Wilcox	Baptist
Harper Grove*	Morengo	Methodist & Baptist
Kemp Grove	Clark	Baptist
Shiloh	Morengo	Presbyterian
St. Paul	Wilcox	Baptist
Thomasville	Wilcox	Baptist

* Public, but supported by Methodist and Baptist

Due to the dependency on farming and other menial sources of livelihood, boys and girls (coming along with the writer's father and mother) in the 1890s and early 1900s received a minimal amount of education—first through fourth grades. Some received no education and could not read or write—not even their names. A select few young men and women completed junior college at Selma University and Payne University, both in Selma, Alabama, and became teachers at the expense of all other family members primarily supporting them. Many of the school-age boys and girls born between 1905 and 1915 had better opportunities for schooling, enrolling in high schools located in Thomasville and Annie Mainie. Still, most did not complete elementary school.

RISE OF LUTHERAN SCHOOLS IN ALABAMA

Rosa Young was a prime pioneer in establishing parochial schools in Alabama. She operated a little school supported financially by individual donors. In 1915, incoming funds were not sufficient to support her school. Upon writing and appealing to Dr. Booker T. Washington of Tuskegee Institute for help, she was directed by him to bring this urgent matter to the attention of the Lutheran church for its consideration. The letter from Miss Young to Lutherans was written from Neenah, Alabama, October 17, 1915, as follows:

Dear Friend:

I am writing you concerning a school I have organized. I began teaching here in 1912 with seven pupils in an old hall, where the cattle went for shelter. Since then I have bought (with money collected in the community) five acres of land and erected a four-room schoolhouse thereon beside our chapel, which we are working on now; bought 45 seats, 5 heaters, 1 school bell, 1 sewing machine, 1 piano, a nice collection of useful books, and 150 New Testaments for our Bible-training Department.

I am writing to see if your Conference will take our school under its auspices. We will give you the land and the school-building, and all its contents to start with. If you cannot take our school, I beg the privilege to appeal to you to give us a donation to help us finish our new chapel. No matter how little, any amount will be cheerfully and thankfully received.

This school is located near the center of Wilcox County, twelve miles from the county seat, fifty-four miles from Selma, Alabama, two miles from the L & N Railroad, amid 1,500 colored people. The region is

*very friendly; both white and colored people are inter-
ested in this school. I hope you will see your way clear
to aid us.*

> *Yours humbly,*
> *Rosa J. Young*

The Rev. Nils J. Bakke was appointed by the Rev. C. F.
Drewes to investigate the matter. Upon investigation and
evaluation, Bakke approved and recommended that Miss
Young's school be supported by the Lutheran church.
Within a few months after Bakke's arrival as the first missionary pastor for the Easter service in 1916, 58 persons
were baptized and 70 persons were confirmed. Shortly
thereafter 14 additional persons were baptized and 43
more were confirmed, totaling 185 people. The congregation was named Christ Evangelical Lutheran Church,
Rosebud (Wilcox County), Alabama. Sponsored by the
Lutheran Synodical Conference, the school at Rosebud
became a Lutheran parochial school in 1916 and was
regarded a model for establishing numerous other
parochial schools throughout central Alabama.

The writer attended the Good Shepherd School at
Vineland. He had been out of school the whole year prior
to the beginning of the Lutheran school in Vineland
because there was no public school in his geographic area
for African Americans. My parents sent us by car 12 miles
one way to a Baptist parochial school before my forced-out
year; yet after one year of travel expenses, my parents were
unable to send us six siblings at home to school. My first
encounter with Good Shepherd at Vineland was attending
a Christmas program. I was nine years old, and this was the
first time I had heard the Christmas story and Christmas
carols. Four of us siblings enrolled in the Vineland Lutheran
School. This was a great turning point in our educational
and spiritual lives. Not only did we learn reading, writing,

and arithmetic, but also religion as well as language usage, health skills, music appreciation, history, and geography. The school was not the customary three- or four-month school, but seven months in duration, plus two or more weeks of summer school when farms were "laid by."

Black boys and girls did not have the privilege of being bused to school free-of-charge as did their white counterparts. They were neither allowed to attend public schools with white children nor to ride the beautiful yellow buses with them, not even for short distances, although the buses picked up white children in areas where black children lived. Many black children walked to Lutheran parochial schools long distances over treacherous roads because there were no public or private schools of any significant value in many areas where numbers of blacks lived. For example, the writer walked to Good Shepherd Lutheran School four miles each way primarily on a small path through the woods including some makeshift crossings over branches (small streams).

There were numerous boys and girls who received their basic education in Lutheran parochial schools. Although most of them did not graduate from the local schools, they learned the valuable truths of the Christian religion, basic life-survival skills, and enough fundamental academic education to get along in life. A total of 23 schools from which data is available and seven others without any existing records served boys and girls in Alabama. (See Table 1.)

As indicated in Table 1, between 1938 and 1983, 23 or more Lutheran parochial schools in Alabama were discontinued. A major factor in this situation was the cost of operation and teacher salaries. Lutheran teachers in Lutheran schools were compelled frequently to seek better salaries in public schools to meet their personal high cost of living.

Other factors for closing Lutheran schools were the opportunities, accommodations, and availability of attending public schools which seemed to be better equipped with necessary resources and could afford well-qualified teachers. Mobility of rural people to urban communities for better living and job opportunities was of significance also.

In spite of the challenging factors indicated above, a large number of African American children still attend Lutheran parochial schools. According to "Lutheran School Statistics," there were 15,573 black enrollees in elementary, high school and other educational facilities during the 1992-93 school year. With the 35 districts of The Lutheran Church—Missouri Synod reporting, six percent of the 255,333 enrolled in elementary, high school, and other special schools are black students. Although many of the parochial schools have ethnic identities, Lutheran schools are becoming more and more multicultural with whites, blacks, Hispanics, Asians, Indians, and others. The large majority of Lutheran students are white—83 percent, leaving 17 percent nonwhites of various cultural and ethnic groups.

Presently, there are still nine Lutheran parochial schools comprised of African American children in Alabama. They are identified in Table 2.

Table 1

Name	*Place*
Christ	Rosebud
St. Andrew	Vredenburgh
St. James	Buena Vista
Mt. Carmel	Midway
St. John's	Joffre
Our Savior	Possum Bend
Bethany	Nyland
Grace	Ingomar
Zion	Tatt's Place
Our Redeemer	Longmile
Bethlehem	Holy Ark
St. Peter	Pine Hill
Holy Cross	Camden
Bethel	Rock West
Gethsemane	Hamburg
St. Luke	Lamison
St. Matthew	Arlington
St. Mark	Ackerville
Peace	Maplesville
St. Philip	Catherine
Messiah	Bashi
St. Timothy	East Selma
Good Shepherd	Vineland

Total 23

Year Started	Year Highest Attendance	Year Discontinued
1916	50 in mid 1930s	1963
1917	40 in mid 1930s	1957
1917	60 in mid 1930s	1963
1917	47 in 1938	1949
1917	20 late 1930s	1949
1917-1918	106 late 1930s	1963
1918	47 in 1939	1965
1918	84	1938
1920	49 in 1938	1952
1922	50 late 1950s	1963
1922	62 mid 1930s	1958
1923	35 in 1940s	1965
1925	89 in 1960	1963
1925	63 in 1939	1963
1925	29 in 1940s	1965
1926	41 in 1942	1965
1926	27 mid 1930s	1965
1927	18 mid 1930s	1963
1928	17 in 1934	1971
1928	54 in 1940s	1965
1929	56 in 1942	1983
1932	80 in 1950s	1970
1931	46 in 1934	1965
(1916–1932)		**(1938–1983)**

Note: Four schools for which data is not available were Pilgrim, Birmingham; Faith, Mobile; Trinity, Selma; and St. Paul, Oak Hill.

Table 2

Location	School	Pre-School	Elementary
Arlington	Epiphany	X	K–8
Atmore	Ebenezer	X	—
Bessemer	Zion	X	K–4
Birmingham	Pilgrim	X	K–4
Mobile	Faith	X	K–3
Mobile	Mt. Calvary	X	K–7
Mobile	Trinity	X	K–4
Montgomery	Trinity	X	K–6
Tuscaloosa	Holy Cross	X	—

MOVING AHEAD

The former Alabama Lutheran Academy, now Concordia College, is the direct result of the pioneer Lutheran work done in Alabama.

In 1919, at a conference held in Midway, near Miller's Ferry, a resolution was adopted to petition the Synodical Conference for funds to build a school for the special purpose of training professional church workers. The location selected for the new school was Selma. The first classes were conducted in a rented cottage at 521 First Avenue, November 13, 1922. The Rev. R. O. L. Lynn was the first president. The first buildings on the present campus were dedicated by the director of missionaries, C. F. Drewes, on September 20, 1925. One year later, four women made up the school's first graduating class. God continued to bless this new Alabama school and made survival possible during the Great Depression.

Significant changes in the school's history are the following:

1. The Synodical Conference transferred the entire ownership and operation of the school to The Lutheran Church—Missouri Synod in 1962.

2. The name of the institution was changed from Alabama Lutheran Academy and College to Concordia College in 1980.

3. The school received full accreditation from the Commission on Colleges of the Southern Association of Colleges and Schools in 1983.

4. The school was granted permission by The Lutheran Church—Missouri Synod to advance to a four-year degree-granting institution in 1989.

5. Four-year college certification was granted Concordia by the Southern Association of Colleges and Schools in 1994.

Concordia College is positioned to be the leader in black Lutheran education. For the first time in this century, the proportion of blacks living in the South has increased. In 1988, 56 percent of the black population called the South home. Concordia can help provide the many more pastors, teachers, and other professional church workers who are needed to reach the expanding black population with the Gospel and positive Christian values. By the year 2000, The Lutheran Church—Missouri Synod plans to begin 100 new black ministries. Today, there are only 52 black pastors available for full-time service to existing congregations; less workers are available to serve new congregations. Foreign countries are requesting increasing numbers of black mission developers. By the year 2020, nearly 17 percent of the people in the United States will be black.

Overall, one can conclude that the Lutheran parochial schools of Alabama serve as mentors, role models, and "springboards" for many other parochial schools in various sectors of the United States, and as sight-lifters for Christian young men and young women as they pursue academic excellence at Concordia College, Selma, and other institutions of higher education in near and faraway places.

On Sunday, July 25, 1993, a service was conducted in Rosebud, Alabama, commemorating the faithful work of Dr. Rosa J. Young to the glory of God. Dr. Young was a pioneer in establishing Lutheran schools and churches to help African Americans. Approximately 150 people gathered in and around the school-church building established under the leadership of Dr. Young in 1916. The writer presented the sermon on "Showing Compassion" based on Matthew 9:38. Only the application of the sermon pertaining to the Lord's compassionate servant, Dr. Rosa Young, is reiterated below.

A Tribute to Rosa J. Young

May 16, 1874–June 30, 1970
First Missionary to Bring the Lutheran
Church to the Black Belt

My dear fellow pastors, teachers, former church members, former classmates, former students, sisters and brothers in Christ:

On April 30 of this year, I took it upon myself to visit this Rosa J. Young memorial. I came all alone—all by myself to see it with my own eyes. I beheld this church school facility and walked around on these hallowed grounds for more than an hour. As I did so, the sacred words infiltrated my mind: "Surely the LORD is in this place"; "Put off your shoes from your feet, for the place on which you are standing is holy ground." (Gen. 28:16; Ex. 3:5 RSV).

How true! For it was here that the Lord used Dr. Young as an example in showing compassion to multitudes of black people in Wilcox County, other sectors of Alabama and this country, and distant parts of the world.

I

Nearly 1900 years after Jesus' earthly ministry, Rosa J. Young picked up her cross and followed Jesus along the road of compassion. She looked upon the hundreds of black people in Wilcox and adjoining counties and saw their miserable plight. Illiteracy was rampant, morality was in decay, and spirituality was enshrouded with darkness. As a young teacher, she had compassion on the people and often said, "I want to do something to help my race." She begged, borrowed, and sacrificed to establish a school for black children in Rosebud, a rural community in Wilcox County, Alabama. While this facility was being erected, she held her first classes in a cattle stall. It was after this facility was completed that classes were held here. Many other communities called for her help to bring education and enlightenment to their black children.

Your speaker for today was one of those children who was a recipient of Rosa J. Young's help in education and enlightenment. I was nine years old when I attended a Christmas program at Good Shepherd Lutheran School in Vineland. For the first time, I heard "Silent Night! Holy Night!" For the first time, I heard "O Little Town of Bethlehem." For the first time, I heard "Hark! The Herald Angels Sing." For the first time, I heard the meaning of Christmas—that in the city of David, Bethlehem, Jesus our Savior was born. For the first time to know it, I heard John 3:16: "For God so loved the world, that He gave His only begotten Son, that whosoever believeth in Him should not perish, but have everlasting life."

Like myself, there were multitudes of blacks in por-
tions of Alabama that were literally lost and reaped from
the Lord's compassion through Rosa J. Young. This woman
brought education and the light of the Gospel to many of
us who were victims of illiteracy and spiritual darkness.

II

In Rosa J. Young's time, there was the need for more
workers. As people heard of her effective service in behalf
of black people in Rosebud, people in various communities rallied around the Macedonian call, "Come over ... and
help us." Mission schools started popping up all around as
popcorn from a hot greasy frying pan. We learned about a
number of places we never heard of previously. "Who had
heard of Possum Bend? Who had heard of Rock West? Who
had heard of Ingomar?"

The missionary woman traveled extensively to initiate
and start Alabama Lutheran schools and churches.
Sometimes on wagons, mules, and other times she walked.
On at least one occasion she walked 15 miles. Once in a
strange area, no one would give her sleeping accommodations. She sat on the side of a road and cried. A woman
passerby asked her about her problem. The missionary
woman replied, "The foxes have holes, and the birds of the
air have nests, but I know not where to lay my head." The
woman had pity and invited her into her home.

Rosa Young prayed for help. Sometimes, her prayers
and tears extended into long hours and sleepless nights.
The Lord responded with additional workers for the
schools and mission churches. There was a Rev. Lang. There
was a Rev. R. O. L. Lynn. There was a Rev. Peter Hunt. There
was a Rev. Marmaduke Carter. There was a Rev. Charles
Peay. There was and is a Rev. Albert Dominick. These were
only a few of many workers. In keeping with the times, I
am pleased to tell you that there were faithful women

teachers. There was a Chineta Smith-Riley-Lawhorn. There was a Mable Smith. There was a Bernice Smith. There was a Julia Jenkins. There was a Delores Smith at the Academy in Selma. During Rosa J. Young's era, there were 33 mission churches and/or schools besides a large number of preaching stations.

After World Wars I and II, large numbers of African Americans migrated north, west, and east to their expected "promised land." As immediate results, there were the St. Philips—St. Philip in Chicago—St. Philip in Detroit—St. Philip in Cleveland, and other St. Philips established in various sectors of the country. After a while, people learned that there were other names for churches such as St. Paul, St. Peter, and putting the name of the congregation last as the Lutheran Church of the Resurrection.

III

Rosa J. Young was a restless woman for saving souls—her own and others. When she was young, she was restless because of her impoverished, faltering spiritual condition and her zeal to help others in need—trying to do it by herself. But as she was more mature, having learned and believed in the power of Christ as her Savior revealed by the Holy Spirit through the Word of God, she was restless in endeavoring to bring knowledge, enlightenment, and the light of salvation to black children and adults. It appears that somewhere she read of St. Augustine's prayer, "Thou has made us for Thyself, and our souls are restless until they find their rest in Thee."

We should know also that Rosa J. Young was a humble and appreciative person. On one occasion while I was at our Selma school about 30 years ago, some of the persons at a meeting kept calling her "Miss Young." I rose to sensitize those present that she was "Dr. Young," and encouraged them to so honor her since the church through one of its institutions had seen fit to bestow such an honor on her. After the meeting, she walked up to me and shook my hand, saying, "Thank you! Thank you very much!"

If Dr. Young could speak to us today, she would not want such recognition and tribute that we are showing her on this occasion. Perhaps, she would say, "I did what I did by the grace of God through faith in our Savior Jesus Christ." The words of the hymn writer I believe express her sentiment very well:

> *But drops of grief can ne'er repay*
> *The debt of love I owe;*
> *Here, Lord, I give myself away*
> *'Tis all that I can do.*

Those of us who believe in Jesus Christ and know His compassion and who honor Dr. Young, a self-giving mentor and model, would do well to repeat:

> *But drops of grief can ne'er repay*
> *The debt of love I owe;*
> *Here, Lord, I give myself away*
> *'Tis all that I can do.*

REFLECTIONS SUMMARIZED

1. Lutheran parochial schools made a significant contribution in providing basic education to hundreds of educationally deprived African American children in rural areas of Alabama.

2. Hundreds of adults as well as children received spiritual enlightenment through the biblical instruction and other religious resources of the Lutheran schools in Alabama.

3. Lutheran schools served as a base for establishing churches which preached the Word of God that made people wise to salvation through faith in Christ

Jesus and administered the sacraments as divinely instituted.

4. Lutheran schools became a springboard for students to pursue further education in high school and college toward productive vocations and professions.

5. Lutheran schools, through the power of the Scriptures and the Holy Spirit, served to motivate hundreds of young men and women to enter the pastoral and teaching ministry; some of these are writers of this book.

6. Lutheran schools in the south provided "seed" and resources for establishing schools and churches as people migrated to eastern, northern and western sectors of the United States.

7. The vast majority of African American leaders in the Lutheran church past and present are products or by-products of Lutheran parochial schools.

8. Present and future Lutheran schools are sincerely and seriously to consider the multicultural make-up of enrollment and curriculum in learning and teaching for making disciples of all nations (Matt. 28:19), irrespective of race, color, culture, national origin, sex, or socio-economic status.

9. The Scriptures in Lutheran schools give a completeness to the curriculum and the teaching-learning process involving children and youth in becoming both knowledgeable in the academics and wise to salvation (2 Tim. 3:15).

10. Christian education in Lutheran schools is a vital enabler to children and youth to be like the youthful Christ and grow "in wisdom and in stature, and in favor with God and man" (Luke 2:52).

Bibliography

Dickinson, Richard C. *Roses and Thorns.* St. Louis: Concordia Publishing House, 1977.

Johnson, Jeff G. *Black Christians: The Untold Story.* St. Louis: Concordia Publishing House, 1991.

Lutheran School Statistics. St. Louis: The Lutheran Church—Missouri Synod, 1992-93.

Noon, Thomas R. "Rosa Young's Letters to Tuskegee." *Concordia Historical Institute Quarterly,* Fall, 1992.

Phillips, Ulrich B. *Plantation and Frontier Documents.* New York: Burt Franklin, 1910, 1969.

The Right Tool. St Louis: The Lutheran Church—Missouri Synod, 1988 (video).

Young, Rosa J. *Light in the Dark Belt.* St. Louis: Concordia Publishing House, 1950.

100 Years in a Nutshell. Black Lutheran Centennial, n.p., 1877-1977.

1992 Statistical Yearbook. The Lutheran Church—Missouri Synod. St. Louis: Concordia Publishing House, 1993.

SUGGESTED ADDITIONAL READINGS

Clark, K. B., and M. P. "What Blacks Think of Themselves." *Ebony,* November, 1980.

Horton, Myles, and Paulo Freire. *We Make the Road by Walking: Conversations on Education and Social Change.* Philadelphia: Temple University Press, 1990.

Ritter, Bruce. *Sometimes God Has a Kid's Face.* New York: Covenant House, 1988.

Vogel, Linda J. *Teaching and Learning in Communities of Faith.* San Francisco: Jossey-Bass Publishers, 1991.

2

Urban Ministry, the Church's Inescapable Challenge

Richard C. Dickinson

It seems important to preface this section with two sources of knowledge that were necessarily utilized: 1) information gained from both my undergraduate courses and graduate studies, and 2) recollections from personal experiences cited throughout the chapter to enliven the message.

In 1957, while pastor of Mount Calvary Lutheran Church, Kannapolis, North Carolina, I took advantage of the opportunity to go back to college and complete my undergraduate degree. We black pastors had not been required to have an undergraduate degree to enter the seminary at Immanuel Lutheran Seminary, where I received my theological education. For my undergraduate degree at Barber-Scotia College in Concord, North Carolina, I majored in social studies. One of the required courses for my major was "Rural Sociology." It was an interesting course and also an easy course for me since I had been raised on a farm in rural Alabama. Moreover, I had five years of pastoral ministry behind me, all of which were done in rural Alabama and North Carolina. In my course of rural sociology, neither the author of the textbook nor the instructor wasted any time or space talking about how the customs, traditions, rules, mores, and total culture of rural life in America evolved. The student was left to assume that this is the way that rural life had always been, and that this is the way that rural life will always be. In this course the roles of the home, the church, and the school were clearly delineated. Their primary task was to know and to respect the fundamental rules and customs of the rural culture. No one was expected to question any of the customs, rules, values, and judgments of the rural way of life. They seemed to have been valued as having been handed down to us by Moses from the hand of God on Mount Sinai. These rules of conduct, this rural culture and way of life, had seemingly been taught by the home, the church, and the school for thousands of years. The Negro spiritual says, "Give me that old time religion. It was good for the Hebrew children. It was good for Paul and Silas. It was good for my old mother, and it's good enough for me."

The course could have led one to believe that one of the givens of rural culture was that rules and regulations, customs and traditions, and ways of life were established by God Himself, and one of the basic attributes of God is that He does not change. Did He not say in Malachi 3:6, "I am the Lord, I change not"? But the church that will seriously consider the challenge of *urban ministry* must know and accept the hypothesis that one of the major constants in *urban society* is change. On the one hand, it is not good to put a value judgment on the issue of change, for not all change is bad. On the other hand, not all change is good, but for good or for bad—for better or for worse, the urban society is in constant flux. Today's answers become tomorrow's problems. It is like how the people say the weather is in St. Louis, "If you don't like our weather, just wait a little while and it will change."

In my second semester at Barber-Scotia, I took an elective course entitled "Social Problems." I wanted to know which problems could creep in and upset the well-structured, orderly, and peaceful rural society which I had learned so much about in the first semester. There should not be many deep-seated problems in a culture which had proven to be so effective for thousands of years. I discovered that these problems existed in such issues as crime and poverty, divorce and welfare, racial and ethnic discrimination and conflict, labor and management conflict, social stratification, the cultural and communication gap between young and old, discrimination of women and minorities in the job market, and the list goes on and on.

In 1967, I was in a doctoral program and attended the Urban Training Center at the Chicago Theological Seminary, and the University of Chicago. The courses which I studied in this program caused me to conclude that the course "Social Problems," which I had studied at Barber-Scotia, was only an introduction to a course in urban sociology and/or urban ministry. Each of us in the program took what was called "the plunge." We spent three days and nights on skid row with little or no money. We learned about the culture, the values, and survival systems of these persons who had given up on society. The individual who was willing to listen and not always ready to pontificate about some moral principle could learn much from these people. Many of them had at one time reached the very top in their professions, but they were suffering from what we today call burnout. Living on the street with these people, it did not take long for one to fall in love with them, to become adapted to their way of life, even to become hardened to some of their immoralities (e.g., shoplifting and stealing). I remember being told when I was very hungry that I could get a good meal at the Salvation Army, but I would have to sit through a very boring sermon first. I must say that the food was delicious and the sermon was not boring.

As another part of the course, we toured and studied Robert Taylor Homes on State and Federal Streets. In this high-rise housing complex lived about 80,000 people within 20 blocks between 35th and 55th Street. It is one of the most densely populated places in the United States. It is one of the largest concentrations of urban poor in the world. There were so many social problems in this high-rise concentration of Robert Taylor Homes that I came away convinced God never intended that humans should live together like sardines in a can. Population density is a major issue affecting some social environments, and nowhere else in the world is this more clearly seen than in Robert Taylor Homes.

At the time of the above experiences, I was a pastor of a congregation in the Chatham community, which was a bedroom community of middle-income black people. The community had recently changed from white to black residents. The racial membership of Chatham Fields Lutheran Church at that time was about 80 percent black and 20 percent white. I think that there were more interracial couples in that congregation than in any other in our church body. In a culture like ours, these couples have many problems that are peculiar only to them. Just a few blocks south of the church building, the systematic block-by-block expansion of the black ghetto was keeping racial tensions at the boiling point. Gang activity was so open that the Blackstone Rangers gang went around in uniform and played football on the midway of the University of Chicago. Back at Chicago Theological Seminary we talked about all of the above situations and issues in the urban society and their relevance to the ministry of the church. I was suffering greatly from culture shock and longing for the good old days when life was much simpler, and the culprit of change was always complicating a simple and happy way of life.

RURAL SOCIETY TO URBAN SOCIETY OVERNIGHT

It is abundantly clear to me that the rural patterns and the rural way of life which have dominated this planet since before the dawn of recorded history have been supplanted by urban patterns and urban ways of living. The existing social problems plaguing us today are manifest in the natural resistance to the swift and sweeping changes which urbanization naturally produces. It is a slow and tedious process which naturally changes a culture. When that process is greatly accelerated and stages or steps in the natural process are shortened or omitted or bypassed, conflict is the natural result. To effectively change the social patterns in the culture and also have them readily accepted by society usually takes several generations; however the sweeping changes forced upon us by today's rapid rush to urbanization all over our nation and the world have happened in essentially one generation. At the beginning of the 20th century, the population of the United States was 85 to 90 percent rural. At the beginning of the 21st century, the population of the United States will be 85 to 90 percent urban. The rate of change is even greater in many developing countries.

The revolutions in transportation and communications, the sweeping improvements in technology which have enabled industry to locate in small towns, the advances which have brought electricity, gas, water, telephone, television, and other "city services" to the rural areas—all have worked to bring the urban culture and ways of life to the rural areas of America. Today, whether one lives in the city or in the country, he is still influenced by the way of life which we usually find in the city.

I like to reflect on rural Alabama, the haunts of my childhood, to see the many changes which have taken place over the years. Now, residents have electricity, natural gas, telephones, and water meters just like in the city. None of these were there when I was a child not too many years ago. Most people have automobiles for transportation, and the faraway places of my childhood are just around the corner for the rural dweller of today. I was amazed recently that a group in my hometown was getting ready to go to Atlanta, about 300 miles away, to see a Braves baseball game, and would be back and ready for work the next day. Modern expressways have made such speedy trips possible. One of my old playmates sits in his air-conditioned home and watches television by satellite and can pick up all of the stations which one can see in the city.

Urban culture, with all its social problems, has become a way of life today, and all evidence confirms the assumption that it is here to stay. How the church responds to the social problems resulting from the sweeping changes that urbanization naturally fosters is the most important issue of our day and time.

Urbanism is a way of life. The city is a settlement of socially heterogeneous people. There is a correlation between the size of the population aggregate, the density of the population, and the heterogeneity of the people. Increasing the number of inhabitants in a town beyond certain limits will have noticeable affect upon the relationships between people. Increasing the number of inhabitants of a community beyond a few hundred is bound to limit the possibility of each member of the community knowing all the others personally. In my little rural hometown we were taught to always speak to everyone that we met. The men tipped their hats to the ladies. Just think of how impossible this is to do when you are meeting hundreds of people all through the day!

THE URBAN LIFE IS A LONELY LIFE

In the rural culture one has to know more and more about less and less. In the urban culture one gets to know less and less about more and more. The song which states "I want to go where everybody knows my name" directs me back to my childhood. I was raised in a rural area of Alabama where everybody really did know my name, and for miles around I needed only to mention my mother or my grandfather, and I would be recognized. In the city it is not unlikely that your next door neighbor for many years may not know your name. If the population aggregate is increased to hundreds or several thousands, the possibility of each person knowing the other personally is greatly limited and soon becomes impossible. This does not mean that city dwellers have fewer acquaintances than do the rural folks, in fact they may have more, but it does mean that of the acquaintances and friends they have less intensive knowledge. If one wants to go where everybody knows his name, he wants to live in the rural society of old.

In the 1930s and 1940s there was a radio program called "Broadway, My Beat." The officer who introduced the program from the "Great White Way," where hundreds of thousands gather and traverse daily and the business never ceases, teaming with activity 24 hours each day, called this place the longest mile and the loneliest mile in the world. It reminds one of The Rime of the Ancient Mariner where it reads, "Water, water, every where, And all the boards did shrink; Water, water, every where, nor any drop to drink." When a person in that kind of society looks around, he is surrounded and inundated by people, wall to wall people, and nobody knows his name. It seems that the essence of urban society is to remain forever Mr. and Mrs. Anonymous. In this densely populated conglomeration of humanity, people are very reluctant to develop close relations. They prefer a very detached way of life. They are the society of the unknown and the unconcerned.

Somewhere in almost all urbanites in this lonely crowd is the desire to be someplace where they are accepted, where they are persons, significant participants with other people who call them by their names. The church should structure its ministry to try and provide for this crying need of the lonely crowd. I am not a great supporter of the mega-church concept. I believe in small congregations of 300 more or less. The mega-church can provide for the needs of the lonely urbanites by providing for many circles of friends within the large circle of congregation. Many in the lonely crowd are looking for a circle of friends small enough to know and to be known.

The church could organize around some of the crying needs of people and the social problems resulting from the pressures of urban living. The church could organize a singles club for the lonely hearts and give Christian young men and women a place to go to find Christian companionship. Why should our young ladies have to go to bars to find companionship? The church could have volunteer service groups for those who have lots of leisure time on their hand and would like to do something good and needful. Talk with any of the old faithful members in the congregation and almost always they can point to some board, committee, auxiliary, or club in that church which is active enough to use their talents and small enough that each person knows all and everyone knows each other by name.

THE TRADITIONAL FAMILY—A CASUALTY IN THE URBAN WAY OF LIFE

A crippling casualty of the urban revolution is the traditional family, which was the chief cornerstone of the rural society. In the typical rural society, the father was considered the primary breadwinner, and the mother and children supported him in this role. The mother was considered the primary homemaker, and the father and children supported her in this role. In that system the father usually made the decisions about the farm and other external matters. The mother usually made the decisions about the home and other internal matters. Both mother and father came together to make decisions about the children. The children were expected to obey. A little complaining was usually tolerated, but, in the end, obedience was strictly enforced. It was clear that the mother received the bad end of roles. In addition to helping in the fields, she had to cook the food, clean the house, wash the clothes, and be prepared to do the same all over again and again. This is usually a thankless and endless task. The children gave her credit by repeating this rhyme: "Father works from sun to sun, but mother's work is never done." In this typical rural family, the enculturation of the children was simplified in the fact that much of their education was on-the-job training. They were with one or both parents almost every wake-hour, except when they were in school. Father taught the boys in the fields. Mother taught the girls in the fields and in the home. Relatives and friends counseled and advised when the children were away from home. That was the culture of rural America only a few short years ago, and the people loved it.

Life there was simple, the rules very clear.
The lonely offender must pay very dear.
So love it or leave it, and be on the roam,
The parents have spoken, and they rule this home.

And the children complained as all children do, but with tears in their eyes, they sang the song of John Howard Payne:

> *'Mid pleasures and palaces, though we may*
> *roam,*
> *Be it ever so humble, there's no place like*
> *home. ...*
>
> *An exile from home, splendor dazzles in vain!*
> *Oh! Give me my lowly thatch'd cottage again!*
> *The birds singing gaily that came at my call,*
> *Give me them with the peace of mind dearer*
> *than all.*
> ("Home Sweet Home," 1823)

There are many elders of today remembering that period of yesteryear with nostalgia like the words of the following song:

> *When the busy day is o'er, and the sun is sink-*
> *ing lower,*
> *Then I seem to see a dear old southern home.*
> *And the long years roll away, just a child again*
> *I play,*
> *With my playmates in the woods we used to*
> *roam.*
> *And at eve my mother there listens to me say*
> *my prayers,*
> *And I feel her kiss as in the days of old.*
> *But now mother's old and gray, waiting for me*
> *far away,*
> *Where the sunset turns the ocean's blue to gold.*
>
> *Oh, the old church bells are ringing,*
> *And the mocking birds are singing,*
> *As they sang around the place in days of old.*
> *And though I am far away,*
> *All my heart has been today,*

Where the sunset turns the ocean's blue to gold.
(c. 1902, author unknown)

Longing for the days of long ago is not going to solve the problems of today. We may as well strive to come to grips with the urban problems of our time because, for better or for worse, for richer or for poorer, in sickness and in health, the urban society will be with us until death us do part. Many of the urban problems which we have today are a direct result and/or amplified by the disintegration and demise of the home. The changing roles of the father and mother as breadwinners is simply one of them. Some may say that the terms *disintegration* and *demise* are too strong, but I think that to say anything less is to underestimate the catastrophic effects that the urban way of life has had upon the family. In 1930, there was a ratio of one divorce to every 50 marriages. Today there is a ratio in excess of one divorce in every three marriages. It blows the mind. In 1930, single women with children were by far the exception. They were put on discipline by the church. Last year, in the United States, there were more births to single parents than to married couples, and this figure does not try to include the abortions. The Department of Human Services, as a matter of policy, will not assist indigent families as long as the father is at home. It does not matter that he is hopelessly unemployed. In the black ghetto, this policy alone has destroyed more homes than unfaithfulness and desertion. In the homes which remain, with the husband and wife both working outside the home, sometimes with shifts varying or working so far away that they are able to spend precious little quality time with the children, the burning question which begs for an answer is, "Who is raising the children?"

It is easy to blame the vanishing family for the social problems plaguing us, and there will be much validity to it, but the challenge to the church in ministry is to work to create, establish, strengthen, and solidify good Christian homes. The church will strive to keep them in God's Word so that they may grow in the grace and knowledge of God's way of life for them. The church will plan and work to enable parents and children to spend quality time together on a regularly scheduled basis. The church will be readily available as a support system to help that family in all times of need.

LIVING BEHIND BARS TO KEEP THE CRIMINALS OUT

Another major problem of our urban society is the problem of crime. The jails and prisons are overcrowded, and we are still setting new records for violent crimes every year. One would expect that the criminals would be behind bars and the law-abiding citizens would have the freedom of the streets, but in modern day urban American the criminals appear to have control of the streets, and the law-abiding citizens live behind the bars of their own homes trying to keep the criminals out.

Since the days of Sodom and Gomorrah, the city has been called the den of iniquity, the stronghold of Satan. I don't know the author of the following poem, but it does mirror the thoughts of many about the great city which was my home for many years.

> If you never have altered your name in your life,
> Or never did up to a bar go,
> Or never ran away from another man's wife,
> They won't let you live in Chicago.
>
> Some folks send by Adams Express,
> And others put faith in Old Fargo,
> But if you want to go to the devil direct,
> Just enter yourself for Chicago.

The city with fast gals and gay gamboliers
Is as full as a ship with a cargo.
And it is truthfully said that the very best men
Fight like chickens and dogs in Chicago.

The infants they feed on whiskey direct,
And for liquor they to their Ma go.
And the muly cows give, as some might expect,
Whiskey punch in the town of Chicago.

They won't let the ministers live in the town,
For on him they will put an embargo—
Unless he drinks wine with all his young friends,
And then he may stay in Chicago.
(c. 1890, author unknown)

Another poem which I think appropriate to describe the feelings about the crime-ridden city is as follows:

Stand in your window and scan the sights,
On Broadway with its bright white lights.
Its dashing cabs and cabarets,
Its painted women and fast cafes.
That's when you really see New York.
Vulgar of manner, overfed,
Overdressed and underbred.
Heartless and Godless, Hell's delight,
Rude by day and lewd by night.
Bedwarfed the man, enlarged the brute,
Ruled by crook and rum to boot.
Purple robed and pauper clad,
Raving, rioting, money mad.
A squirming herd in Mammon's mesh,
A wilderness of human flesh.
(c. 1916, author unknown)

The ministry needed in this age when crime and litigation is so vast? That need seems to be endless. There is ministry to the offenders and/or their families. There is

43

ministry to the victims and/or their families. There are programs for the ex-offenders to help them readjust to society. There are programs to keep young people off the streets in the hope that keeping them busy will keep them out of crime and contribute to making them productive of positive good in society. But regardless of all the programs by the church, the schools, and other elements of society, the rate of crime continues to rise unabated, and in fact in many places it seems that the rate of growth has accelerated. To me this is proof that we have not learned how to cope with the urban revolution sweeping our land. We are quick to blame the home for the breakdown, but we are slow to admit that the homes which we are speaking of have all but disappeared from our culture today.

IS CULTURAL INTEGRATION A FACT OR A MYTH?

One of the greatest challenges to the church in urban ministry is the heterogeneity of the urban population. A few of the old cities in West Africa evolved and developed around the kinship group. Their culture has remained relatively constant down through the centuries. Almost all of the cities and metropolitan areas of the western world developed and expanded around commerce and industry. These metropolitan areas have attracted all races and nationalities, all cultures and religions, and people of every tribe and tongue. All professional groupings and social stratification have been drawn as with the pull of a magnet to live and work in the metropolitan areas of our land.

All of these people, the white collar worker and the blue collar worker, the professional and the wage earner, labor and management, must interrelate on the job and in the market place. To interrelate in the urban setting is more or less a surface relationship. Interrelating may be defined as interacting of people with other people in a meaningful and coherent fashion. Usually there is little or no friction in interrelations. Only when one moves from interrelations to integration will one expect resistance. Integration is a much more meaningful and binding action. To integrate is to make into a whole by bringing all parts together, to unify. To integrate into an effective unity, the many parts must be made or adjusted to fit. The great difficulty with integration is deciding who must sacrifice what in order to be accepted, in order to fit. Very often to effectively integrate into a given society, one must learn a new language, a new culture and way of life. Often for the urbanite, to interrelate or to integrate, that is the constant enigma of life.

Not too many years ago the anthropologists and sociologists talked constantly about the creation of an American culture. They called it the "Melting Pot Theory." Conceivably, all the races and nationalities, the cultures and conditions of people from every corner of the globe that came to this nation would contribute a little and sacrifice a lot of their culture, and out of this strange mixture would emerge an American culture. That is what true integration would produce. But the ingredients in the melting pot never melted. One needs only to visit and possibly tour the cities of New York, Chicago, or Los Angeles to discover that immigrants to this country as a rule refused to integrate. They created for themselves little ghettoes, where they live and continue to enjoy and perpetuate their race, ethnic identity, language, and culture. Some of these ghettoes, like Chicago's Chinatown, have well-defined boundaries, and they have existed for many generations. In Chicago's Chinatown many Americans of Chinese descent, born in America, live to a ripe old age and never learn the English language. Other ghettoes are always expanding, shrinking, or relocating. Frankly there is hardly any racial, ethnic, or cultural integration happening in this type of society.

At one time there was reason to believe that there could and possibly would be cultural integration of Americans of European descent such as Germans, Scandinavians, English, Irish, Polish, Italians, and others, but the third generation of these immigrants is trying to restore the ethnic cultures of their foreparents. It is called the third generation thesis: "The third generation wants to remember what the first generation wanted to forget." African Americans are experiencing this third generation affect today. When I was a child, to call someone black was to ask for a fight. Today, not to call that person black might be asking for a fight. There is just as much cultural pluralism in the African American, Hispanic, and Asian communities today as there is cultural pluralism in the communities of the Americans of European descent. W. E. B. DuBois correctly predicted that the problem of the 20th century would be the problem of the color-line. I will predict, and I believe rightly so, that the problem of the 21st century will be cultural pluralism. If our nation can master this enigma, it can rightly lead the world. If the church can master this, it will hasten the day when the Gospel will be preached to the ends of the world.

All of the above issues have great relevance to the church in mission and ministry. As a rule, the church which an individual joins is determined more by sociological factors than by theological affirmation. Only after a person has been gained for the kingdom and thoroughly indoctrinated in the faith can we say with any degree of validity that he or she is a member because of the teaching of the church. It is easy to underestimate the profound affect of the church upon the culture and of the culture upon the church. The church has truly had a most profound and powerful affect upon the culture of this nation. The opposite is also true. The customs, traditions, values, and laws of the culture and of the church have become so intermingled and intertwined that as one judges them, it will be most difficult to determine what is purely theological and what is purely sociological in nature and in origin. One must remember, however, that man as a psychological and a sociological being is inextricably intertwined. Adam communed and communicated with God and everything was good, but remember, it was God that said that it is "not good" that man should be alone. We may conclude from the book of Acts that the church which tries to minister to people in their own language and culture according to their most recent needs will doubtless be the most effective. In the biblical record of Pentecost in Acts 2:6-8, we read, "Now when this was noised abroad, the multitude came together, and were confounded, because that every man heard them speak in his own language. And they were all amazed and marvelled, saying one to another, Behold, are not all these which speak Galileans? And how hear we every man in our own tongue, wherein we were born?" Then the record lists about a dozen nationalities. I think that it is very meaningful that the record of Pentecost reads this way. It is a diverse world into which the Lord has sent His church. He wants the church to take the cultures and conditions of people seriously. As the apostle Paul says, "I have become all things to all men, that I might by all means save some" (1 Cor. 9:22 RSV).

I was constantly in culture-shock in Nigeria, West Africa, where there were 394 separate languages. Of course each language has some distinct differences in the culture of the people. I remember one day that we traveled through 10 separate language barriers on a 30-minute trip. But upon returning home, I discovered that a person does not need to go to a foreign land to discover the multiplicity of language barriers. I went to Los Angeles on business and discovered that the area surrounding the airport had become a ghetto. One truly needed to know the Korean language to secure effective service in restaurants.

To minister successfully to this racially, ethnically, and culturally diverse mixture of humanity, the church must learn to effect unity in diversity, to achieve unity and not insist upon uniformity. This challenge is not easy, for one needs to be able to distinguish the theological from the sociological. One dares not teach for doctrine the commandments of men. But what is even worse, one dares not treat God's Word as if it was the word of man. Luther is quoted as having said that when a person is able to rightly divide the word of truth so well that he can rightly distinguish between Law and Gospel, that person is a good theologian. I will say that when a person is able to rightly distinguish between theology and culture, that person should make a good missiologist. The church body which must insist upon uniformity of doctrine in the midst of a multiplicity of cultures is in critical need of that good missiologist.

Bibliography

Dubose, Francis M. *How Churches Grow.* Nashville: Broadman Press, 1978.

Fava, Sylvia Fleis, ed. *Urbanism in World Perspective: A Reader.* New York: Thomas Y. Crowell Company, 1968.

Glock, Charles Y. and Rodney Stark. *Religion and Society in Tension.* Chicago: Rand McNally & Company, 1965.

Grams, Armin. *Changes in Family Life.* St. Louis: Concordia Publishing House, 1968.

Halverson, L. W. *The Church in a Diverse Society.* Minneapolis: Augsburg Publishing House, 1964.

Keesing, Felix M. *Cultural Anthropology.* Chicago: Holt, Rhinehart and Winston, 1965.

Lee, Robert. *Cities and Churches.* Philadelphia: The Westminster Press, 1962.

Lueker, Erwin. *Change and the Church.* St. Louis: Concordia Publishing House, 1969.

Riesman, David. *The Lonely Crowd.* New Haven: Yale University Press, 1977.

Webber, George W. *God's Colony in Man's World.* Nashville: Abingdon Press, 1960.

Witt, Raymond H. *It Ain't Been Easy, Charlie.* New York: Pageant Press, Inc., 1965.

SUGGESTED ADDITIONAL READINGS

Hale, Russell. *The Unchurched: Who They Are and Why They Stay Away.* New York: Harper & Row, 1980.

"Homicide Records Set in 22 Cities." *USA Today,* December 29, 1993.

Mead, Loren B. *The Once and Future Church.* New York: The Alban Institute, Inc., 1991.

Myers, Walker Dean. *Now Is Your Time! The African American Struggle for Freedom.* New York: Scholastic, Inc., 1991.

Neuhaus, Richard John. *Unsecular America.* Grand Rapids: William B. Eerdmans Publishing Company, 1986.

"200 Million Guns Can't Be Ignored." *USA Today,* December 29, 1993.

3

Worship in the African American Church

William H. Griffen

The topic of worship in the African American church is very broad, since there are various types of African American churches, many of which have varying forms and styles of worship.

There are African American churches or congregations that are members of mainline Protestant denominations— that is, denominations that have their roots in Europe. Congregations in the African American community that have this background have worship styles that resemble that of their mother denominations, though in recent years this has begun to change. Moreover, there are the so-called "historic" African American churches. These churches belong to denominations that were organized by African Americans and to this day serve the largest number of African Americans. This chapter will be concerned with these churches rather than the mainline Protestant denominations, because most of the readers are familiar with the former and less familiar with the latter. Before we begin to look at the specifics of worship in the African American tradition, we want to speak of worship in somewhat general terms.

MEANING AND TRADITION OF WORSHIP

The word *worship* describes a common experience of the believer. It is not only a noun in the language of the believer, it is a verb as well. It is the name given to something Christians do. The emphasis is on the doing. Worship then is action.

Worship has been an important part of the life of the believer from the beginning. Adam and Eve worshiped God even before the Fall. After the Fall, Genesis tells us that God came "walking in the garden in the cool of the day" seeking Adam and Eve. It is my view that this was not the first time that God had come walking in the garden. It appears that as God came to them, Adam and Eve had communion with God or worshiped God. We know that God created humans in such a way that they are to be in communion with him. I believe that this communion with God was worship. Adam and Eve saw God as the creator and themselves as the creatures, and thus they worshiped God.

Even after the Fall the worship continued. Abel worshiped as he brought offerings to God. Noah worshiped God after the flood, and we see many examples of Abraham and the other patriarchs worshiping God. So from the very beginning, worship has been a vital part of the life of those who believe in God. The psalms, which someone has called the hymnbook and prayer book of the Old Testament, are filled with worship expressions; therefore we conclude that God is the center of our worship.

The New Testament also contains significant hymns. We see some of them in the Gospel of Luke—Zechariah's song at the birth of John the Baptist and Mary's song when she was told she would give birth to the Savior. There are some songs in the epistles of Paul. It may be that Philippians 4 is a hymn that was sung in the early church. Likewise, the victory hymn over death in 1 Corinthians 15 has been regarded as an ancient hymn of the church. So, in both the Old and New Testaments, worship was vital to the life of believers.

The word *worship* in English is a very old word. It can be traced back to an Anglo-Saxon word, *worthship,* a word used to attribute worth to something. The word was *worthship* at first, but over the years it became *worship.* The word *worship,* when used in a religious context, means "ascribing worth to God."

Since we speak of worship as "worthship" and the giving of honor and reverence to God, this is quite true in African American worship as well. This concept is obvious in the music of the African American church, especially in its gospel music.

There are many gospel songs in the African American church which pick up the theme "worthship." Among the Gospel songs that speak of worthship are such titles as "He's Worthy" and "Oh, Magnify the Lord with Me." Gospel songs such as these can be found in the works of the Rev. James Cleveland, Andrae Crouch, and the Winans, just to name a few of the well-known gospel music writers and singers. Their works can be found in almost any African American collection of gospel music. (See, for example, *Lead Me, Guide Me: The African American Catholic Hymnal.*) These songs are sung as a part of worship as a way of indicating that we worship God because He deserves to be worshiped. He is worthy of worship.

In all Christian churches, including African American congregations, it is the excellent worthiness of God which makes our worship possible. When we worship Him in church or in private family devotions or in personal devotions, the thought that is uppermost in our minds and hearts is that God alone is worthy, and it is He that we worship.

In his book on worship, the Rev. Terry Dittmer gives us a list of words that describe worship. He presents an acronym to describe it, namely N.E.R.V.E. Worship according to Dittmer is *natural, expressive, reverent, voluntary,* and *emotional.* Each of the words describes Christian worship.

EXPRESSIVE AND EMOTIONAL WORSHIP

The two words that will be discussed here, specifically pertaining to African American worship, are "expressive" and "emotional." Both of these words are a vital part in all worship services, but they become a very special focus in African American worship.

The term *expressive* means that worship is something that we do, we have a way of expressing ourselves in our worship in various ways. Some of these ways are: we stand for the confession and reading the Gospel, bow our heads or kneel when we pray, speak words with our mouths, kneel at the altar for Holy Communion, and make upon ourselves the sign of the cross. All of these demonstrate that worship is expressive. We find ways to use the members of our bodies in worship.

In African-American worship we see other modes of expressiveness. When the choir is singing a selection that is especially meaningful to the worshipers, the worshipers may join in the singing, stand to show assent, clap their hands, or do body movements. Expressiveness in African American worship is also seen in the clapping of hands and even shouting to indicate dialog with the preacher. All of these are expressions of worship.

The second word that specially describes African American worship is "emotional." Some people are afraid or maybe even ashamed to show their emotions, especially in worship. But I heard a black preacher tell his congregation that since God gave us our emotions we should not be afraid to use them. Our emotions are as much a part of us as our minds.

Most Lutherans seem to minimize the use of emotions in worship. They appear to have the opinion that to be emotional is unintellectual, as if the two are in conflict with each other. Lutherans obviously demonstrate that worship is to be cognitive, that it is to appeal only to those who are intellectual enough to comprehend/participate. That is quite natural for Lutherans. I once heard someone say that the Lutheran church is cognitive because it was born in the university, and another said that it stayed there. We should not be afraid of our emotions. They can be a valuable asset in worship. Worship at its best is intellectually and emotionally satisfying as well.

We see emotions as a vital part of African American worship. Feelings are important. It is true we do not base our faith on our feelings or emotions; they are indeed fickle, and we attempt to point that out to people. We want them to understand that feeling good is not necessarily a proof that people are believers or that they have the Holy Spirit. We want them to come to appreciate the wisdom of the person who said, "Be my feelings what they will, Jesus is my Savior still." We can know that Jesus is our Savior no matter what we feel, and that truth is bound to bring good feelings.

Some criticize the showing of emotions in worship because they feel that those who do are trying to draw attention to themselves rather than focusing attention on God. This may indeed be the case in some persons, but as the preacher said, God gave us our emotions, let us use them to the fullest in worship.

There are several ingredients in worship. These are music, liturgy (including prayer), and preaching. We want to look at each of these in terms of African American worship.

MUSIC IN WORSHIP

One of the most important elements in African American worship is music. Someone quoted Dr. Martin Luther as saying that the devil hates music. This may or may not be true. I think it is more true to say that the devil hates some types of music. There is music that the devil loves. Much of the music we hear in society today is causing the devil to have a field day and through it gain many converts. When we listen to some of the lyrics, we can conclude that the devil is making good use of music to win and keep converts.

This is not the case with black religious music. Music is a vital part of the African American worship experience. In most societies music plays a major role in a person's religion. This is especially true in African American worship. There is no question that black sacred music has been the glue in the survival of the black religious experience.

It is a well-known fact that much of the African music came from African life. Despite the inhumane and oppressive treatment under which African Americans lived during slavery as well as many years after slavery, African Americans have not forgotten their African heritage. One of the reasons for this is music. Despite the calculated and premeditated designs to sever all historical relationships and to root out all memory of the African experience from our ancestors, some of the music and other African expressions survived. So we find a striking parallel in form and survival of Africanisms in African American sacred music.

Not only did its music keep heritage alive, it was music that has sustained and nourished the African American church and African Americans in general despite the inhumane imposition of laws and the oppression and injustice African Americans faced.

When we consider African American sacred music, we need to be reminded that all music inclusive of sacred music reflects the social context of the times in which the music is developed. This was true of the music of the Lutheran church. Since this essay will be read by Lutherans, I take this opportunity to give examples from the history of the Lutheran church. Take a look at the hymns that were written during the time of the Reformation, and you will see that the hymns, lyrics, and the scores are warlike in nature. They are reflecting the times. We can gain a good understanding of the Reformation by studying the hymns that grew out of that era. Or if we take a look at the hymns under the theme of judgment in *The Lutheran Hymnal* and the dates they were written, we will discover many of them were written during the Thirty-Years' War and have themes such as suffering, death, and the end of the world.

It is no wonder that African American sacred music reflects its social context. If we look at the sacred music that grew out of slavery, namely the Negro spiritual, we see that this is true. Or, if we look at the music that grew out of the Great Depression of the 20s and 30s, namely Gospel music, we still see the reflection. If we observe spirituals which were changed during the time of the Civil Rights Movement of the 60s, we see that the themes reflect liberation from racism and oppression. Sacred music in the African American tradition, then, is judged on how well it helps African American people resist a social condition of racism and oppression.

In considering the Negro spirituals in this context, we need to keep in mind that the Negro spirituals served a two-fold purpose: they dealt with the evils of the society of that day, and they were protest songs. They spoke against the oppression African Americans were experiencing. There were code songs that were designed to bring about rebellion against the system. The strongest form of rebellion was that of escape from slavery and going north. At the same time, the songs were spiritual in nature. We see an example here:

> *Steal away, steal away, steal away to Jesus.*
> *I ain't got long to stay here.*

This spiritual was, on the one hand, a code song announcing that one of the "conductors" of the underground railroad was near and those who wanted to leave should steal away to the hiding place because the train "conductor" would not be there very long. On the other hand, it could mean spiritual closeness to Jesus.

Another familiar spiritual is "Go Down, Moses." This may have been a song that talked about a famous "conductor" who went by the nickname "Moses." Harriet Tubman had come to take the slaves out of "Egypt," a nickname for South Carolina, to the promised land, Canada.

It is also quite possible that spirituals could be sung during a worship service with spiritual meanings. A significant number of Negro spirituals speak of rivers. Some suggest that this is because the slaves remembered the long and arduous journey across the ocean to the shores of this land and related the ocean to a deep river. "Deep River" is such a spiritual. In it, the slaves speak of going over Jordan and longing to go to camp ground. The camp ground they meant may have been their native Africa. Some of the slaves, however, may have been thinking of the camp ground as being heaven. If this is true, they seemed to have recognized the need to pass through water before entering into that camp ground. Since the slaves had seen Baptisms at rivers, they could have also been referring to Baptisms, believing that it is through Baptism that one passes over into the promised land.

Another such spiritual that had double meaning is "I'm So Glad Trouble Don't Last Always." Trouble was never far from the consciousness of the slaves; it could come on them in a moment's notice. Singing this song may have been a way of surviving the trouble they were experiencing in the present, or it could have been a prayer for deliverance from the trouble they would receive in the afterlife.

Thoughts of the end of the world and of the second coming of Christ were never far from the consciousness of the Negro slaves. This may have been because life for the slave was often fragile and uncertain. The possibility of death was always near, which may explain why so many of the spirituals deal with the subject of death and the coming of Christ. They would often sing, "I want to be ready to walk in Jerusalem just like John."

"Good News, Good News, the Chariot Is Coming": this spiritual was used by many of the slaves to announce the coming of persons connected with the underground railroad to deliver them from physical slavery. That must have been good news. Some slaves seemed to see a deeper meaning in these words, because they knew that there was not only physical slavery but spiritual slavery as well. They may have longed for a chariot that would come and set them free from this slavery also. They no doubt remembered the chariot that carried Elijah to heaven and may have longed for one to come and take them there as well.

One of the better known Negro spirituals is "Come by Here." It is sung at youth gatherings and at campfires as a folk song. Many sing it without thinking of its message. The spiritual is a prayer. It asks the Lord to come to visit one who is in trouble. The spiritual speaks of someone crying and of someone praying in time of need. The spiritual is a fervent prayer to God to come with help. But again, the spiritual may have a code in it. The code may have been telling the slaves one of the "conductors" in the underground railroad is to come this way, that it is safe to come, or that there is a group of slaves ready to go on the way to freedom.

There are two other points that I want to make concerning spirituals before I leave them. The first is that the spirituals are biblically based. The spirituals refer to both Old Testament and New Testament characters. "Joshua Fit the Battle of Jericho" is from the Old Testament, and "Oh, the Blind Man Stood on the Road and Cried" comes from the New Testament.

Many of the spirituals deal with the power of God rather than the grace of God. This is understandable; the slaves saw their weakness, so they focused on the power of God to deliver them from danger. One such spiritual is "My God Delivered Daniel, and if God Delivered Daniel, He Can Surely Deliver Us from Our Condition."

It is not surprising then that the spirituals have lasting value in African American worship. They deal with the real human conditions and troubles that still exist in the African American community, as aforestated, reflecting the times of present-day oppression as well as hope for the world to come.

A second type of music widely used in the African American churches at the present is gospel music. Gospel music began on the south side of Chicago under the leadership of Dr. Thomas Dorsey. He is called the father of gospel music. One of his most famous creations is "Precious Lord." It was made even more famous because it was one of the selections sung at the funeral of Dr. Martin Luther King a number of years ago.

When gospel music was introduced in the church in the early 1920s, it faced much resistance. It was considered too worldly and not fitting for worship. This was true of spirituals as well. Bishop Payne, a black pastor trained at a Lutheran seminary, felt the same way 100 years earlier concerning Negro spirituals. It was his position that spirituals should not be used in worship. Thank God he did not prevail.

The same happened to Mr. Dorsey in his development of gospel music. Thomas Dorsey said that the early rejection of gospel music by some in the church made him even more determined to make it useful for worship services. Those who opposed gospel music for use in the African American church failed also, because over the years it has become very popular in the African American church.

Another criticism of gospel music is that it is too humanistic and too subjective. Those who subscribe to this position point to the lyrics of many gospel songs as not giving glory to God for His goodness, but rather to human response to God's goodness. Those who make this criticism of gospel music need to look at some of the psalms. Many of the psalms talk of the writer's personal relationship with God, and much gospel music does the same. Also, many of the psalms were written in the first person. This would seem to indicate that this is an appropriate way to praise God even in corporate worship.

Another feature of gospel music is, like the spirituals, it adheres very closely to the biblical text. Many times the lyrics are drawn directly from the Bible text itself. Consider this example of Psalm 27, phrased by Lillian Bouknight.

> *The Lord is my light and my salvation!*
> *The Lord is my light and my salvation!*
> *The Lord is my light and my salvation!*
> *Whom shall I fear? Whom shall I fear?*
> *Whom shall I fear?*
> *The Lord is the strength of my life. Whom*
> *shall I fear?*

It is noteworthy that like the spirituals, gospel music also places much emphasis on the power of God. It is the opinion of this writer that African Americans dwell on the theme of the power in gospel music for many of the same reasons that African Americans dwell on the power of God in spirituals, and we will note that the same is true in much of the African American preaching.

We gave the above examples of gospel music for the reader to perceive how appropriately and true the summary statements mentioned above fit into the gospel music.

A third type of music used extensively in African American worship is metered hymns—especially the long meter, short meter, and common meter hymns. The metered music African Americans used most often came from the works of Dr. Isaac Watts. His hymns were easily sung in congregations which could not afford a musical instrument. Dr. Watts' hymns are still quite popular in African American worship.

In the early African American churches many of the people could not read. This meant that the hymns were learned from memory. The choir would lead them line-by-line, and the congregation would join in singing them with the choir. In some cases, there was a song leader who would "raise a hymn," lining out the hymn lyrics line-by-line and then singing the line. For example, the leader would speak one line of the hymn and then assist the congregation in singing that line, and then he would go on to the next line until the hymn was sung in its entirety. An example of this is

> *Song leader (spoken):* Alas! and did my Savior bleed?
> *Congregation (sung):* Alas! and did my Savior bleed?
> *Song leader (spoken):* And did my Sovereign die?
> *Congregation (sung):* And did my Sovereign die?
> *Song leader (spoken):* Would he devote His sacred head?

Congregation (sung): Would he devote His sacred
  head?
Song leader (spoken): For such a worm as I?
Congregation (sung): For such a worm as I?

As African Americans became more literate, hymn-books began to appear in the pews, but the presence of the hymnbooks did not change the worship. Many of the metered hymns, spirituals, and gospel music are still sung from memory with a song leader or choir leading the con-gregation.

It is worth noting that the theme of the power of God is not as pronounced in the metered hymns used in African American congregations. However, the metered hymns that were more popular, as determined by their use in African American worship, were hymns that dealt with trials and troubles. This is natural since, as cited above, the hymns and worship of a congregation reflect the social context and the conditions that the people are experiencing, and trou-ble and trials are never far away for most African Americans in this oppressive and racist society.

LITURGY IN WORSHIP

The liturgy in African American worship is quite sim-ple, reflecting the simple lifestyle of the people who devel-oped it. Its simplicity reflects the theology of the African American church concerning forms and practices. It is only recently that African pastors vested in robes. Until recent years, many of them wore business suits, and even now the robes are simple black Geneva robes, although in some congregations the pastors have turned to the use of colors in their pulpit robes.

The worship generally begins with a devotion and is usually led by the deacons. It is a kind of preworship expe-rience, an effort aimed to help the worshipers become prepared for the main worship which follows the devotion. The devotion consists of a hymn or two, followed by a prayer and a Scripture reading. There may be one or two testimonials, then a Scripture reading, closing with one or two hymns.

The worship continues with an elaborate processional, the choir marching in time with a lively gospel song. Then the minister takes his place in the pulpit as the worship leader. After the processional there is a congregational hymn, followed by a prayer and a Scripture. The choir sings a selection, followed by announcements and the offering. Then there is another choir selection, followed by the sermon. After the sermon, there is the invitation or the opening of the doors of the church, a kind of altar call, followed by a prayer and hymns by the choir or congregation. The worship concludes with the benediction.

The choir is one of the key elements of the worship service in the African American church. Much effort goes into it. The purpose of the choir is to inspire and entertain the congregation. Many African Americans attend a church that they are attracted to because of the choirs. Any African American church worth its salt has a good choir and an elaborate music program designed to add much to the worship. While the minister may be dressed modestly as far as vestment goes, this is not true of the choir. They dress in elaborate robes. The choir is used to enrich the worship and is one of the key ingredients in the growth or lack of growth of an African American congregation.

PREACHING IN WORSHIP

The sermon is the highlight of the African American worship experience, and the congregation and preacher know this, though if there is a good choir, the sermon may at times be somewhat lacking. Preaching then is to meet certain criteria: It must be inspirational, informative and entertaining, appealing to the emotions and the intellect of the worshipers. The sermon must deal with the issues that the people are experiencing in their everyday life, or it will miss the point altogether.

Listen to any black preacher in the rural south or urban north, providing he has not been influenced by attending a white seminary, and you will know without any doubt that he is steeped in the stories of the Bible. He may be unlettered as far as theological degrees go, but one certainty is that he knows the Bible and has committed much of it to memory. He tells the stories of the Bible as did the ancient African storyteller who could make the Bible come to life. Even in our day listen to the black preacher in the predominately black denominations, and you will hear the same skill, that of a storyteller using picture language that makes the Bible live in the minds and hearts of the hearers. The black preacher and black preaching in worship help black people identify with God and His people of old.

For instance, attention is called to the people of Israel in the Old Testament, especially their history of slavery. This is so because the issue of slavery directly ties black people today with the people of God in Old Testament times. This identification is not lost in black preaching. While it is true the chattel slavery that black people had to endure in the past has long since been ended, the truth is that even today many black people are still being dehumanized by an oppressive system that in many cases is just as bad as slavery itself. So the preacher can still preach about Israel's slavery in the Old Testament in a way that makes sense to black people today.

The preacher takes a current issue of oppression, either in the community where he is serving or in one that is far away and is known to his hearers. He compares it to the oppression experienced in Egypt. He describes it in vivid terms. He tells how difficult it is for people to live under this oppression. He describes how tough life is and relates this in such a way as to show that just as Israel was required to make bricks without straw, so black people today have been called on to make bricks without straw as well. Such an illustration thus comes alive for black worshipers. He may describe an Egyptian dynasty that saw Israel as little more than slave labor and compare this to the oppressive system today that sees black people as no more than slave labor.

But the preacher always provides hope. And once again he lets the people of the Bible speak of this hope in vivid terms. Perhaps he reminds his hearers that the Lord was on the side of the Israelites and the Lord is on our side today. Then once more he turns to biblical characters in either Old or New Testament to demonstrate how the Lord was on their side. Thus in worship the story of the Bible comes alive through the identification of black people today who are oppressed with the people of yesteryears who were oppressed.

Maybe the preacher wants to speak on a theme—faith, for example—and show what a difference it makes in the lives of people today. Rather than talk about faith in the abstract, the black preacher makes faith come alive by relating how faith made a difference in the lives of biblical people. He calls on the biblical characters to tell the story just as though they were present in the church. He may choose the Canaanite woman as an example and let her tell how her faith made a difference as she related to the Lord—"Even the dogs eat the crumbs that fall from their master's table" (Matt. 15:27 RSV), and through faith, her need was satisfied. Or he may choose the woman who had an issue of blood for 12 years and let her tell the story of how Jesus made the difference in her life and brought her healing. Or the preacher may take an Old Testament character such as Abraham and let Abraham tell the story of how faith made a difference in his life. The point is that the black preacher lets the Bible characters tell the story themselves.

Sometimes the preacher may resort to acting out the character in the chancel itself as he tells the story, demonstrating it with actions and motions and in tones of voice. He may ask the congregation to join in the refrain so as to involve the people in the story. Some may criticize this as entertainment, but it makes the worshipers become participants, active in the worship experience in ways that make a difference in the lives of people, rather than passively sitting and perhaps missing the point altogether.

Just as the theme of power is very much a part of the music of the African American worship, so the power of God predominates in the preaching. This may be because of the heavy Calvinistic influence on the historical African American church, but it is also true because of the social context in which most African Americans live. We live with weakness and lack of power. People living under such conditions will be attracted to a God of power. We want a powerful God who is able to deliver us from our situation. It may well be that it was the emphasis of the power of God in Calvinistic theology attracted most African Americans to the church which emphasized the sovereignty of God as the beginning point in their theology.

Along with the theme of power in black preaching is the theme of hope. The black preacher never wanted his hearers to despair. Regardless how desperate the situation may seem, he continues to hold out hope in the power of God to help. It is this hope that kept black Christians alive and going in the face of so many things that could cause one to despair.

In the African American experience God does not always demonstrate His power in ways that we would like to see Him do this. In such situations the preacher reminds his hearers that this does not mean that God does not have the power to act. In this way, the preacher is careful that his hearers do not lose hope. He may talk about God delivering Daniel, or he may use the words of the three men in the fiery furnace when they told Nebuchadnezzar that God had the power to deliver them, but even if God did not, they would hope in Him anyway.

The black preacher is not afraid to be involved in politics himself and to involve his congregation as well. Partisan political activities often times become a part of the worshiping experience. The preacher takes a stand and announces his support for a particular political candidate or candidates as a part of the sermon. Or he will announce support for a certain action that will impact the African American community in a special way, and he will urge his congregation to follow suit. The preacher may also invite political candidates to speak in the worship service of the congregation to solicit votes.

Many of the readers will be aware of the fact that the African American church led by black preachers were the base of support for the civil rights movement in the 60s. But throughout the history of African Americans, the church and the black preacher have kept hope alive for black people. This was true during slavery as well. It is an open secret that many of the slave rebellions began in the church with black preachers. The slave owners knew that. That is why at the height of many rebellions, black people were not allowed to worship unless a white person was present. The slave owners recognized that the pulpit was a powerful tool in the hands of the black preacher.

But even with a white person present, the black preacher was able to communicate with his hearers in such a way that the white person would miss it altogether. An example of this can be seen from an incident in

Lutheran history in which a black Lutheran preacher communicated effectively with his black worshipers without the white person perceiving what was going on.

In the early history of the Lutheran church's ministry with black people, a white superintendent wanted to move a black preacher from a church in a small town to a smaller rural church and take the small town church for himself. The black preacher did not want to go—but was forced to do so. When he preached his farewell sermon, he chose words used by Paul on leaving Ephesus: "I know … that after my departing shall grievous wolves enter in among you, not sparing the flock" (Acts 20:29). The phrase "grievous wolves" in Rev. Pheiffer's sermon was an obvious reference to the white superintendent. But the white superintendent missed the point altogether, for he said that while the pastor took the text, he did not develop it. The pastor did not have to, because his hearers knew exactly what he was talking about. So the pulpit is a power tool for communicating with people and moving them to action, and the black preacher is not afraid to do this.

This was true in the past and is still the case today in many urban and southern communities where a significant number of black people live. Politicians also know the power of the black pulpit in getting them elected. Most politicians take great pains not to offend the black preacher, and they work hard to gain his support.

Black preaching is evangelistic in nature. The sermon always ends with the pastor "opening the doors of the church" or an "altar call." The reason for this is because there may be persons who are unbelievers (or sinners as they are called) present during the worship service. African American preachers feel that these people need to be offered the opportunity to accept Christ; no opportunity is to be overlooked; the ritual is almost sacramental. I remember being present in an African American church and the guest preacher who delivered the sermon did not "open the doors of the church," or extend or give the invitation. The local pastor was obviously agitated about this and had another minister who was about to take the offering delay the offering and "open the doors of the church" instead.

There is much to be said in favor of this practice. I recognize that there may be some theological reasons Lutherans may not want to do this, but is it not also true that we should use every opportunity to invite and call people to believe the Gospel of Jesus and by the Spirit's power to receive Him into their lives? Is there something wrong about inviting people to come to the altar during the worship service as an opportunity to renew their faith or even acknowledge or confess their faith as a witness for all to see? There is some merit in doing this. This practice has worked well in the worship of African Americans.

Bibliography

Christian, David W., and Walter Schoedel. *Worship Is Celebrating as Lutherans.* St. Louis: Concordia Publishing House, 1990.

Cone, James H. *The Spirituals and the Blues: An Interpretation.* New York: The Seabury Press, Inc., 1972.

Dittmer, Terry. *Creative Contemporary Worship.* St. Louis: Concordia Publishing House, 1985.

Griffen, William H. *Portals of Prayer.* St. Louis: Concordia Publishing House, July 1988, and December 1990.

———. "Our Roots or Future." Unpublished essay presented at the LCMS Black Convocation, Charlotte, 1991.

———. "Black Lutherans." *Lutheran Education* (River Forest, IL: Concordia University), May 1971.

Johnson, James Weldon, and J. Rosamond Johnson. *The Book of American Negro Spirituals.* New York: Viking Press, 1969.

Lead Me, Guide Me: The African American Catholic Hymnal. Chicago: G. I. A. Publications, Inc., 1987.

Lincoln, C. Eric, and H. Lawrence Mamiya. *The Black Church in the African American Experience.* Durham, N.C.: Duke University Press, 1990.

Martin, Ralph. *Worship in the Early Church.* Grand Rapids: William P. Eerdmans Publishing Company, 1989.

The National Advisory Task Force on the Hymnbook Project. *Songs of Zion.* Nashville: Abingdon Press, 1981.

Walker, Wyatt T. *Somebody's Calling My Name: Black Sacred Music and Social Change.* Valley Forge: Judson Press, 1979.

———. "The Soulful Journey of the Negro Spirituals: Freedom Songs." *Negro Digest,* July 1963.

Wilmore, Gayraud S. *Black Religion and Black Radicalism.* Garden City, NY: Doubleday and Company, Inc., 1972.

SUGGESTED ADDITIONAL READINGS

Jones, Amos. *Paul's Message of Freedom: What Does It Mean to the Black Church?* Valley Forge, PA: Judson Press, 1984.

McCall, Emmanuel L. *Black Church Life-Styles.* Nashville: Broadman Press, 1986.

Mitchell, Henry H., and Nicholas Cooper Lewter. *Souls Theology.* San Francisco: Harper & Row, Publishers, 1986.

4
Ministry in a Multiethnic Parish

Kermit H. Ratcliffe

The writer of this chapter served as pastor of a multi-ethnic congregation in East St. Louis, Illinois, for eight years (1974–82). The church was primarily interracial, comprised of whites and blacks. But due to the influx of all sorts and conditions of people and the multiplicity of individual and group differences of members, it seems applicable for this parish to be referred to as being multiethnic.

Multiethnic ministry is unlike any other ministry. It is a ministry that touches people across all race and culture lines. It ministers to people where they are, especially when they celebrate their greatest joys and when they are struggling with the depths of pain and loss. A multiethnic pastor is a leader, counselor, encourager, example, and friend to all nationalities of people in all kinds of circumstances. This kind of ministry is the enormous task for which no pastor has ever been entirely and perfectly prepared.

The writer felt inadequately prepared for the expectations that his integrated congregation had of him as their pastor, because these expectations were quite different from those brought by him to this ministry. The people came from different backgrounds and had varied experiences, and they brought with them different expectations, needs, and understandings of the pastoral role. It comes as no surprise to anyone associated with multiethnic ministry that it is a very stressful and demanding ministry. Developing a clearer understanding of this ministry can become an open door of opportunity for anyone using its activities creatively. My aim in ministry was not to avoid all the stresses and demands as much as it was to understand and use them as an invitation to personal growth, professional competence, and spiritual understanding of my own strengths and weaknesses.

GETTING STARTED

One of the better ideas I found in my ministry was the ability to organize committees around felt needs identified by the congregation. Our day-care nursery and kindergarten programs were the two community outreach programs that the entire membership supported. The whole congregation took an active part in developing the program. The senior members made special donations of monies to the daily operation of the program. They spent many hours volunteering their time and talents to ensure the continuation of the program. The youth volunteered to come in and clean up the floors and yard after school. The entire group felt some ownership in these outreach programs.

We made the ministry a joy and a challenge for the entire community. We were not able to attract many community people to our worshiping services at the beginning. After we had established ourselves as a church for the community and began to reach into the community with our services and caring ministry, we began to attract more and more visitors. We also reorganized a committee to include a friendship circle to greet and welcome new-comers or visitors each Sunday and to sit with the new persons or family they greeted that day. Our Sunday school, Bible class, and worship attendance began to increase.

We also experienced the losses and disappointments of most multiethnic parishes. As soon as the congregation would get a few new stable families assimilated and into the active life of the parish, those families would move away or transfer out. It was very difficult to show a net gain, because many of our people were moving and transferring their membership to other congregations nearer to where they were moving.

GUIDING PRINCIPLES

The writer's ministry of Law and Gospel was greatly influenced by Goethe's nine principles of a well-balanced life. Without these principles applied to life and ministry, it would have been very difficult to perform or accomplish anything on a daily basis. Nothing taught at the seminary had prepared me for this ministry. Hence, the writer called upon the principles of German philosopher Goethe as life-support guides:

1. Health enough to make your work a pleasure.
2. Wealth enough to support your needs.
3. Strength enough to battle difficulties and overcome them.
4. Patience enough to toil until some good has been accomplished.
5. Grace enough to confess your sins and forsake them.

6. Charity enough to see the good in your neighbors.
7. Love enough to move you to be useful and helpful to others.
8. Faith enough to make real the promises of God.
9. Hope enough to remove all fears concerning the future.

In addition to the Scriptures, Confessions, and our constitution and bylaws, we set some definite standards and norms for our ministry and mission. We established an evaluation tool for each organization in the church and for each position that someone held in the congregation. We tried at every level to be Gospel-based in that evaluation process. After hearing the following poem recited at an installation, someone suggested that we adopt it as a preamble to all our committees and job descriptions. It passed unanimously, and we adopted it. The poem, entitled "Love People Anyway," reads as follows:

> People are unreasonable, illogical, self-centered.
> Love people anyway.
>
> If you are good, people will accuse you of selfish, ulterior motives.
> Be good anyway.
>
> If you are successful, you will win friends, false friends, and true enemies.
> Succeed anyway.
>
> The good you do today will be forgotten tomorrow.
> Do good anyway.
>
> Honesty in practice makes you vulnerable.
> Be honest anyway.

The biggest people with the biggest ideas can
be shot down
by the smallest people with the smallest minds.
Think big anyway.

People favor the underdog, but follow only the
top dog.
Help fight for some underdog anyway.

What you spend years building might be
destroyed overnight.
Build anyway.

People really need help, but they may attack
you if you help them.
Help people anyway.

Give the world the best you've got, and you will
get kicked in the teeth.
Give the world the best you've got anyway.

Author Unknown

Even with principles, plans, and evaluation tools to discuss and study, we still had difficulty reaching a consensus. Those who did not participate adequately on a regular basis felt excluded from the decision-making process when it was time to execute programs. Also, there were times when emergencies would arise that gave the groups little preparation time to study the issues involved. Therefore, we worked diligently to minimize the need for emergency large-group decisions. We found that using a smaller committee to focus only on emergencies was a better plan for consistency in ministry.

IDEAS FOR EFFECTIVENESS

In order for multiethnic ministry to be effective over a longer period of time, the pastor must be a person growing in the Word, in faith, in commitment, in dedication. He should encourage the membership of the congregation to keep growing with him. His depth in the Word should be reflected in Bible study, sermon preparation, and in his general visits. The pastor must love people who will not be able to show much love in return. He will have to develop the courage to know that God will be with him and will empower and strengthen him in his efforts to win others as he shares his faith with them. He must be a man of courage and confidence, unwavering in his determination to serve the Lord and His people in love.

The writer found it to be of benefit to have a more experienced pastor around to talk with, to share concerns, and to help make sense of things that were happening. It was important not to feel alone or abandoned in the ministry. As the needs of people were noticed in the parish and the community, I tried to stay in touch with my own feelings and my own strengths and weaknesses. By doing so, I was better prepared to listen and respond positively in any and all circumstances as they were brought to my attention. After dealing with many of the community people and helping them to find their way in life, they would come and render dedicated service to the church. We welcomed them readily, although we had a policy that no one could serve as head of any committee or board who had not been a member for two years or more.

Multiethnic ministry, like all other ministry, can be divisive if the leadership is not keeping a very close watch on the tone and the tenor of meetings and social gatherings. I realized early in my ministry that humor can bring tears as well as laughter, so we made it a habit not to tell jokes at church.

In the parish you can have, as we did, a very diverse group of people. The mayor, superintendent of schools, and police chief may be members of the congregation. This can be a very enriching and rewarding experience—until the parish supports another candidate for office or until the congregation tries to put some evangelical persuasion on a politician to pay attention to the needs of its community.

The idea that church and state should work side by side in the world works well when the membership of the church is in agreement. That is where I found the ministry of the Word (Law/Gospel) to be most effective. A prayer breakfast was used weekly for years to help church and community leaders refocus and to understand each other's functions, roles, and direction. During my entire ministry I tried to use the Law/Gospel approach to settle all disputes, disagreements, and misunderstandings that would arise in either the church or church-community relations. The congregations that I have been privileged to serve had members from the city, local, and state governments as active participants. So we learned to work with members whose political views were different from those of many in the congregation, yet we continued to work together in accomplishing our greater mission. "Terry" (not his real name), a new convert to the Christian faith, experienced some difficulty in accepting the idea of absolute moral standards. His educational background in philosophy and political science convinced him that absolutes did not exist. However, he gave up these views freely after the Watergate convictions, because those great political leaders had broken an absolute moral standard for which they were incarcerated.

PROBLEMATIC CHARACTERISTICS

The multiethnic parish is a mixture of persons eager to hear, learn, and respond to the leading of the Holy Spirit. At the same time, these people are also preoccupied with concerns far from what may be happening in the congregation. The youths face identity-crises and problems. They do not feel they are the people they were meant to be, neither are they doing the things they are meant to do, nor are they where they ought to be. The older people face illness, loneliness, and death. Couples struggle with marriage, child-rearing, divorce, separation. Others are on the edge— longing to believe, but still uncertain. Some are motivated to work for political change, and others struggle to maintain the status quo. There are the formally educated and the self-taught. And there are the devoted believers whose faith has matured through testing. The congregation is a bona fide potpourri of persons, for each of whom Jesus died.

This ministry really has nothing to do with living off the spiritual capital of the past or indulging in a cult of remembrance of glorying in a man who stood up to the powers of his day and getting a vicarious kick out of it for oneself. No, it means much more than feasting on a heritage or going through the routines of religion.

PAST AND FUTURE

After becoming involved in the multiethnic ministry, the writer often had to choose between the inadequate past and an uncertain future of dealing effectively with people. I would inevitably get caught in processes of change which many times could threaten the very life of the congregation. I had to make a choice between the goals of progress, social justice, and freedom when some kind of incompatibility developed among them. Whatever selection I made had to be made quite naturally on the conviction that I had given my life to Christ and His Gospel and for the sake of others. I had taken up my cross to follow the Lord, who created, redeemed, and sanctified me.

Multiethnic ministry brought to my awareness that no society or church ever succeeds in eliminating all its problems. Knowing this, I continued to believe, accept, and proclaim that suffering is part of life and may be used as an instrument of refinement. What is more, one remains mindful of the fact that frustrating and debilitating experiences do not constitute God's last word on these issues. They are never more than penultimate in their significance. The ultimates of the Gospel are the forgiveness of sins, life, and salvation.

Poverty, for example, is often a matter of degree. There is no absolute standard with which to measure such phenomena. Injustice at times carries within it a degree of ambivalence. But both poverty and injustice may serve as means of spiritual discipline and personal growth, for there is more than a casual connection between such troubles and the kingdom of God. It is folly to try to diminish the contrast between the message of the Gospel and the judgment of the world. Our Lord speaks to those who are poor, that is, to those who suffer from poverty and privation of whatever kind these may be. To those who are unfortunate in the eyes of the world, He announces the joys of the kingdom. As the Messiah, Jesus came in fulfillment of promises which spoke of His characteristic mission as consisting of bringing happiness to the afflicted. The multiethnic parish continues this liberating work in imitation of her Lord.

COMBATTING PRESSURES

Some of the most potent weapons in combating the demons that lurk in any social order are those available to the multiethnic parish. The salvation we proclaim is worked out and lived within this world. Accordingly, faith is no optional superstructure to be superimposed on secular relationships and institutions. Instead, it is a power which must touch life seven days a week. Service to the world that grows ever more interdependent and complex is really the only concrete way in which the church can act today in the task of helping to redeem the social order. It has the resources to do so.

The writer felt this pressure many times during those impossible and yet rewarding years as pastor in a multiethnic parish. I am also acutely conscious of the fact that any communicator who wants to improve his listening skills needs to be aware of the risk involved in ignoring the questions which the listener is first asking and first wanting to have answered. But sometimes that risk must be taken. Right answers are of little use if they are given to the wrong question. The pragmatic "how" question must indeed be addressed by the multiethnic pastor. But the theological "what" question must come first, however strong the psychological pressure may be to reverse the order.

The reasons for the pressure to ask the wrong questions first are very obvious. We have come to think of theology as being purely an academic discipline. It can indeed be that, for the academic theologian has his own vital and honorable contribution to make to the life of the church. But a biblical theology can never be merely reflective or academic. It is at heart practical. The New Testament church preached, taught, worshiped, and cared before it did anything else, and certainly before it articulated its reflective theology. The raw materials of practical theology—homiletics, Christian nurture, liturgies, pastoral care—have been there from the beginning. We who exercise the functions of a biblical Christian ministry are therefore not merely dependent on reflective theology. We are ourselves practical theologians, no less theologians because we are practical. We not only apply academic theology to the practice of ministry but also discover it there. Preaching is itself a kind of practical theology. That is why our working ministry can never be content to be merely a skills discipline, concerned alone with the pragmatic and the question "how." The question "what" must precede the answer to the question "how." The theology of ministry must determine its methodology and therefore the nature of the task itself.

PHASES OF ACTION

How does responsible action begin? We as a multiethnic congregation considered six phases: repentance, dialog, examination of the world, self-analysis, growing in God's Word, and action.

First, the process began with *repentance,* both personally and corporately. By grace, we become aware of our selfishness, our evasions, our fears, and our misunderstanding. These we confessed and acknowledged before God and to one another. We saw our sins as more than failures to measure up to our own best selves. Our breaking of specific biblical laws were symptoms of an even deeper problem, a symptom of our primary concern for ourselves, for our prestige, our possessions, and our comfort; a symptom of the tragic gap between our profession as Christians and our lives. To a great extent, changes had not occurred because we had not desired change. We had gone so far as to feel vaguely anxious about our failure to do something about the brokenness of people in our church and community. But we quickly discovered ways of discharging this feeling of guilt when it reached the point of discomfort. Those who work in social service agencies in the community could tell sad stories of middle-class suburbanites who came to do volunteer work. Too often they would come out of a feeling of guilt or personal boredom. Thus, when their personal needs were met by several sessions of work, they became delinquent in continuing their service. Both the agency and the neighborhood people were worse off because of their short-lived efforts.

Repentance is more than feelings of guilt or sorrow. True, repentance may begin there. But it moves on to include a change of mind, a shifting of one's life so that it begins to run in a new direction. The responsible Christian senses the need for becoming as sensitive to the needs of others as he has been to his own needs. This process might begin as he finds himself in the midst of troublesome situations. Responsible action finds it beginning in repentance before God.

Second, the Christian who would act responsibly can engage in *dialog,* including listening and learning. Complex multiethnic problems will not yield to home-made solutions based on pet theories. Parishioners have become hardened to stock formulations of the Gospel hawked at them by street-corner preachers, shouted by revivalists, and peddled in tracts by people at bus stops. A stance of humility and open-mindedness is also necessary. This does not mean forsaking either the Gospel or courage. It does suggest a necessary pedagogical method.

We are describing a Christian who responds faithfully to a given situation. To interpret the situation correctly, it is essential that he carries on more than a monolog with it. Dialog has become an overworked word in recent years. Yet it is necessary. A Christian must enter into dialog with others in order to assess the true condition of the multiethnic scene. This is a necessary first step toward effecting change.

Below the writer suggests four marks of a dialogical person. 1) He is, first, a total, authentic person. He is never one who uses a situation or other people for his own ends. He enters into the circumstances of life wholeheartedly, with heart as well as mind; he listens as well as speaks. 2) He is an open person. He is willing to reveal himself as well as have the sensitivity to receive the revelation of the other person. 3) The dialogical person is disciplined; that is to say, he is able to assume responsibility for himself and for others. He is able to accept the limitations as well as the opportunities which relationships offer. One's own contribution must be made in the context of the contribution of others in the multiethnic community. 4) Finally, the dialogical person is a related person. Because he is able to respond to others, he can become responsible. He becomes one through whom God can work. As Howe says simply, "It is imperative, then, that a Christian be a dialogical person through whom the Word that gives life is spoken."

The third phase has to do with *the examination of the world.* One is to realize that the arena of God's concern is much broader than any "religioius" sphere. The Christian is opposed to false religion, for the Scriptures are vociferous in their denunciation of any religion which enthrones idols in the place of God. The question to consider therefore is this: Where are the idols in modern religious life, the idols which have usurped the place of God, perhaps while retaining His name as a pious subterfuge?

There are two real worlds: the secular world and the world of faith. Each has its own values, goals, and styles of life. We fear that the false religionist has created a third world, the world of religion. It is an artificial world, where secularism thrives under the guise of symbols of the faith. It is not the world of faith; it is a form of this world that is destined to pass away. It is idolatrous, for it seeks people's loyalties. It is deadly, for too many are unable to distinguish it from the true world of faith.

We should not equate this world of religion with the organized church. While "organization" and "institutionalization" have become dirty words with which to castigate the church in recent years, the problem is not this simple. The moment a group of Christians decide to do anything together, some form of organization becomes inevitable. While this is not the problem, it is true that institutionalized churches become a chief source of that illegitimate world of religion. God eventually becomes the distant symbol behind real estate, buildings, programs, organizations, and projects that may have little bearing on the community or upon faith.

God's concern is about the world He made, that world which has fallen into sin, but a world which He loves and has redeemed in Christ Jesus. God calls people to faith in order to enter that world with His Word of life. He commissions His people to enter that world with service. They go bringing a Word of judgment and a Word of grace. They go hearing a voice different from that of the world; their lives of love are to attest to this.

As a fourth phase in deciding upon responsible action, we made a *self-analysis* of the congregation to determine at what points a change of policy and action was necessary in order to be of truest service to the multiethnic parish and community. The situation will vary with each church. We found that as a congregation we had fallen into patterns of thought and action in which routine had replaced conscious thought regarding the role of the congregation in its community and city. Patterns of life were perpetuated which were no longer effective. They were often designed for a group of people and a social setting that no longer existed. Forms of polity, role expectations of the ministry, methods of outreach, areas of church involvement in the community, and the corporate image the congregation unconsciously proclaimed to its area were badly suited for performing the mission of the church and of faith. Between individual change in the Christian and desired change within the multiethnic community lies change within the thought and structures of the local congregation.

Fifth, *growing in God's Word.* Christians who desire to act responsibly in mission in a multiethnic setting need to be in conscious dependence on God's power as it is conveyed through God's Word. Luther once spoke of the church as the people of God united in the Word of God. The Word is not restricted in some static or fundamentalistic sense to the Bible. It is the total Word of God—preeminently the incarnate Word in Jesus Christ; also the written Word conveyed through the sacramental water, bread, and wine; and the living word as it is spoken by men today. This Word initially imparts life to people; it continues to mold and shape their lives: their thinking and their actions.

Thus while the Christians must live out in the world much of their life of "faith active in love," they must continue to withdraw in order to refuel themselves with the Word. We described the necessary rhythm of assembly and dispersion. In the assembled state, Christians are strengthened for their task in the world. Enthusiasm for service must never endanger the people's spiritual life by sanctioning their separation from the source of life in God's Word.

The sixth phase, *action,* follows. In moving out in faith to our communities, problems were often clearer than solutions. Therefore many of our actions were tentative and experimental. But a beginning was being made. There was a danger that the problems would prove to be so large that they would appear insoluble and as a result could paralyze us into a helpless state of doing nothing. Flexibility did remain important. Those of us who were making significant contributions to the multiethnic ministry tried many approaches. When one would lead to a dead end, we simply dropped that approach or modified it. But we continued to act.

Action was needed on several fronts. Many of the services needed were done by individuals. Mary would volunteer to look after the children of a family when a mother was hospitalized. John developed a city-wide literacy program. Bobby, one of our high school students, after serving as a vacation Bible school teacher's aid, developed a summer school program for the youth of the community that became a year-round program. This program received grants which enabled the youth to go on camping and hiking trips during the entire year. James, the church's custodian, took the initiative to gather together a group of his neighbors to clean up the alley behind their property; this, in turn, started a program of rat eradication in the community.

In a natural way these individual actions flowed into group actions. Georgia organized the program of literacy so that not only one person but scores of individuals were taught to read. As more people were involved and more resources were needed to attack problems properly, higher levels of organizational skills were needed. As the programs grew, a staff person was employed to direct, coordinate, and train volunteer efforts. At the same time, public services were being cut. In order to be heard by the decision-makers of city government, many citizens had to join together to represent a large enough number of voters so that politicians would take specific requests seriously.

Our Lord had sent us to a world that was different from any we had known before. But it remains His world. Therefore, we were to be there. We were to work with hope. For we were the people through whom the Lord would reign in this part of His world, this multiethnic community.

FUTURISTIC CHALLENGES

We stopped and surveyed the situation. A closer look at the community disclosed that it contained more people than when the church was built. We saw human need. And we planned for the future, because God had placed us in the multiethnic community to make disciples, baptize, and teach. We had not only gone to the multiethnic community, God obviously had moved the multiethnic community toward us. With vision and trepidation, often with more commitment than knowledge, we chose to serve the people who lived in the community of the parish.

Perhaps the most dramatic step we took was to make the decision that we were God's voice to all the people of the community, regardless of racial and ethnic differences, family background, social standing, moral standards, police records, whether working or lifelong recipients of relief. When our congregation began to grow in numbers and progress financially, some of the leaders began to feel apprehensive toward the less fortunate. They wanted to establish some restrictive policies on membership. We commissioned a committee on caring and sharing to sponsor a 12-week Bible study seminar for leaders of the congregation. The seminar was a process of carefully teaching the doctrine and purpose of the church.

By the end of this seminar the congregation had installed a wheelchair ramp, had purchased a public announcement system for the church and cry rooms, and had developed a tape ministry for the shut-in members. The congregation had become an inclusive rather than an exclusive parish. For a church that had been a tightly knit, homogeneous group, representing primarily persons of one type of national and financial background, such a change evidenced the work of the Spirit.

The decision to reach out to the community is faced not once, but repeatedly. When the goodwill of the congregation is tested by vandalism, when attacks are made on people in the community while involved in church service, or when the realization dawns that little fruit is harvested in proportion to the fantastic efforts expended, our decision is challenged.

Still, our congregation has continued to respond to the needs around it. For example, we discovered that there were youngsters in the community who were handicapped all of their lives because of poor reading ability. Perhaps half of the teachers in the local school system failed to meet the minimum requirements set for teachers. We responded by opening reading clinics and providing tutors to work with youngsters after school. We initiated a work-study program and then recruited workers from every available source. We found that juvenile gangs had taken over some of the roles vacated by families. But the gangs were becoming destructive. The rumbles and inter-gang fights led to stabbings and thus to arrests by the police. Then we stepped in and gave the gang a place to meet. We knew we were not going to make altar boys out of most gang members. Having some understanding Christians who had lived through gang life in their own youth made it easier to reach out to them as fellow human beings, with no ulterior motives. A few pastors with great patience also established a working relationship of trust with us and the local gangs.

Our community was in desperate need of counseling services. Some other churches joined us in arranging for a team of people drawn from psychology, psychiatry, law, medicine, and social services to come to the church one evening a week to meet those seeking help. The ones who came had been encouraged by others who had been helped. The church had made prior contact with the local hospital, mental health clinic, family counseling service, pharmacists, special training schools, and the like. Since the average person in the lower strata of our community was either suspicious of such groups or unaware of their existence, the churches had to provide the immediate service of listening to problems and indicating where help was available. Since no other social agency was equipped to handle their needs, the churches utilized their resources to provide the needed service. We quickly learned that it would be poor stewardship to try to set up a parallel set of structures on a denominational basis.

FREEDOM TO SERVE

Because of what God has done for us in Jesus Christ, because we are justified by His grace through faith in His promise which promise is Christ, God's great "yes" and "amen," we are free to serve God and other people. We are free to do all God wants us to do, free to love as He loves with no respect of person, the kind of love that seeks the good of others. We are free to help each person to have dignity as God's child, to accept people whether their hair is straight or curly, simply because God has accepted them and empowers us to do the same. We are free to tear down walls that shut people off from other people, free to rejoice in every good gift the Father sends, to accept His discipline and thus be patient, to share our goods since we have received the good of God, especially His mighty acts in Christ which set people free. That is the impelling, liberating power of the Gospel. The Gospel empowers us to live responsibly to God in seeking the good of others, never mind what happens to us here, since we are the Father's children whom Christ will not disown and whom He is not ashamed to call His brethren.

90

Luther caught this freedom of the Gospel, a freedom that is free from human opinions, free from rules that would tyrannize and enslave, when he said, "The Christian is the most free lord of all, subject to none." And yet it is never a freedom of irresponsibility or selfish pleasure, a doing whatever you want whenever you please no matter what, never a freedom turned into license.

Yes, Christ has set us free from every power that would tyrannize, brutalize, and destroy, from sin and death and hell, from self and the favor of others. It cost Him dearly; the cross cost Him His life as He gave total obedience to His Father in the face of every temptation to do otherwise, and He gave it for us all. This crucified and risen Lord, who rules over all and for all who love Him and look for His appearing, authorizes us to love and serve in His name. In His authority we have our freedom, for we are free when we serve Him, and we are slaves again when we quit. Therefore, we can venture forth into each day expectantly in the freedom of Christ's rule. That is what it has meant for me to be a pastor in a multiethnic parish.

Bibliography

Barna, George. *The Frog in the Kettle: What Christians Need to Know about Life in the Year 2000.* Ventura, CA: Regal Books, 1990

————. *The Master Plan of Evangelism.* Old Tappan, NJ: Fleming H. Revell Co., 1987.

Dawson, John. *Taking Our Cities for God: How to Break Spiritual Strongholds.* Altamonte Springs, FL: Creation House, 1989.

Galloway, Dale E. *20/20 Vision: How to Create a Successful Church.* Portland, OR: Scott Publishing Co., 1986.

African Americans and the Local Church

Garlow, James L. *Partners in Ministry: Laity and Pastors Working Together.* Kansas City, MO: Beacon Hill Press of Kansas City, 1981.

Lueke, David. *Evangelical Style and Lutheran Substance: Facing America's Mission Challenge.* St. Louis: Concordia Publishing House, 1988.

Money, Thomas. *Basic Communities: A Practical Guide for Reviewing Neighborhood Churches.* Minneapolis: Winston Press, 1984.

Reeves, Daniel R., and Ronald Jenson. *Always Advancing: Modern Strategies for Church Growth.* San Bernardino, CA: Here's Life Publishers, 1984.

Ott, Stanley E. *The Vibrant Church: A People-Building Plan for Congregational Health.* Ventura, CA: Regal Books, 1989.

Schaller, Lyle E. *It's a Different World.* Nashville: Abingdon Press, 1987.

SUGGESTED ADDITIONAL READINGS

Schuller, Robert H. *Your Church Has a Fantastic Future!* Ventura, CA: Regal Books, 1986.

Tillapaugh, Frank R. *Unleashing the Church.* Ventura, CA: Regal Books, 1982.

Tregoe, Benjamin B., John W. Zimmerman, Ronald A. Smith, and Peter M. Tobia. *Vision in Action: Putting a Winning Strategy to Work.* New York: Simon & Schuster, 1989.

Wagner, Peter C. *Spiritual Power and Church Growth.* Altamonte Springs, FL: Strang Communication Co., 1986.

92

5
Church Work in Rural Communities

Robert H. King

Hush! Hush! Somebody's calling my name;
Hush! Hush! Somebody's calling my name;
Hush! Hush! Somebody's calling my name;
O my Lord, O my Lord, what shall I do?

The words of this spiritual seem to depict the desperate cry of numerous African American rural churches of the past and appear to indicate the agonizing spirit of some of the few that still exist. Moreover, the problem of survival of rural churches is general in scope and has to be reckoned with seriously in various sectors of the United States.

A major concern in the last decade approaching the 21st century is the diminishing image and function of church work in rural communities. Evidences of concern are seen in fewer active rural congregations, others struggling to survive, and still others literally dying or disintegrating. Interested churchmen and churchwomen are addressing the concern by conducting church leadership conferences, course work in seminaries and other institutions of higher education, workshops, discussion groups, video- and audiocassette productions, and others. More and more attention is given this matter in a variety of books and publications. Church statistics are providing increased data on the present and futuristic appearance of smaller churches. Generally, many rural churches seem to lack numerical growth, dynamic stability, and genuine care and understanding support from parent church bodies. Even less backing seem to go toward rural churches with a bleak outlook for self-maintenance, positive growth, and visible development toward their future survival.

The purpose of this chapter is to focus on Lutheran rural churches that have African American makeup, orientation, and/or relevances. Specific questions addressed are the following:

1. What are some of the problematic concerns of African American rural churches?
2. How have societal changes affected African American churches?
3. How may practical directives serve to offer positive objectives to African American rural churches?

PROBLEMATIC CHANGES IN RURAL LIFE

A variety of progressive changes have been encountered by African American rural people for more than a half century. Some of these changes were traumatic and challenging, while others fostered a better way of life. Factors influencing changes are the following:

Outdated traditional farming

Technology

Economy

Family life

Mobility

Armed services

Technical/educational training

Professional and/or vocational opportunities

Outdated traditional farming techniques have become less and less effective. The typical African American farm averaged 30 to 80 acres for growing crops, raising cattle, maintaining forestry for firewood and timber. Plowing with mules or horses, hauling with wagons, milking cows by hand, manual hoeing, and using two-man crosscut saws for sawing wood and timber became things less used on small farms. The same happened with families who were sharecroppers, farmhands, and renters of land and houses from landowners.

Technological machines and devices emerged as the thing of the day, such as tractors for plowing and hauling, cotton pickers, corn pullers, milking machines, chain saws for sawing wood and timber, fish ponds for growing fish, and raising cattle for sale and for family food. In addition, electric lights, refrigerators, deep freezers, and inside-plumbing for cooking, washing, and bathrooms became available to farm families who could afford such useful accommodations.

Economic insufficiencies made it impossible for a large number of African American families to have many of the technological means available. Meager incomes from the farm and common labor were not sufficient to make life more livable through the offerings of technology. Poor farm families were outstripped by more affluent farmers and ambitious businessmen striving to get ahead and able to take advantage of economic and technological opportunities.

The family life of rural African Americans was put into shambles by emerging technological and economic changes. With the small family farm forced into exile by technology and economic pressures, members of the family found themselves scrambling to secure a livelihood. This affected the traditional extended and corporate family

95

styles. Family members had to leave home in small segments of two or three persons, joining small bands of relatives and friends in various urban areas of the country for a better way of life. Some also went into the armed services as a way of self-support; others pursued educational and technical possibilities through federal and other sources; still others through federal, state, and other assistance sought preparation and training to secure higher types of professional and vocational positions with comparable salaries.

Mobility to urban areas eased somewhat the economic pressures of rural life experienced by African American families. During World War II and the Korean War, young men and women as well as some middle-aged persons sought and found wartime employment in factories, plants, and companies engaged in producing war materials and equipment as well as items useful on the home front. Such mobility added to the diminishing of the small farms.

Armed services themselves also had mobilizing affects on weakening small farms. Younger men and younger women were called to active duty during World War II and the Korean War. Many of the small farms were almost nil by the time of the Vietnam War, which called young men and women to serve upon the beckoning call of the United States government.

Technical and educational opportunities during and following the wars produced an upward mobility for African Americans. In the armed services, some soldiers were privileged to pursue a trade or develop a vocational skill such as auto mechanics, truck driving, secretarial office training, medical assistance, cooking, leadership training, group dynamics, graphics, music, and others. Educational prospects were made available following experience in the armed services. The GI Bill of Rights and other veteran programs offered high school and/or college education to GIs. They pursued professions in religion, teaching, medicine, law, science, agriculture, and others. Vocational pursuits were made by others in upholstery, bricklaying, carpentry, forestry, cattle raising, and a variety of shops and small businesses.

Professional and vocational opportunities led trained, qualified persons to jobs in various sectors of the country, both urban and rural. During the last 25 years, a large number of jobs have been secured in companies and corporations established in large rural areas in the south. Men and women have been able to use their skills and competencies in nearby geographic areas as well as in northern cities. Some have also pursued employment opportunities abroad, particularly in Africa, Europe, and Asia. African American scholars have walked through the doors of some of the most prestigious institutions of higher learning, including Harvard, Yale, Columbia, the University of Chicago, Cornell, and others.

EFFECTS OF CHANGES ON RURAL CHURCHES

The societal changes encountered by rural African Americans did not only affect their personal everyday lives but also their spiritual lives and their churches. From the writer's own experiences, verified to a large extent through research, by observation, and from pertinent recorded data, the writer identifies effects of changes on rural Lutheran churches as follows:

1. Self-determination shattered.
2. Insecurity overwhelming.
3. Worthlessness envisioned.
4. Lovelessness realized.
5. Conquer or escape as choice.

Many rural church people experienced a *shattering of self-determination* as a carry-over from the overpowering changes in their lives on small farms. Farming with mules and horses, wagons and plows, hoes and swing blades, cutting wood by crosscutting saws and axes, and other similar items became obsolete. People had used the preceding means to do for themselves. They exercised their own abilities, skills, and strengths to actualize self-determination and self-realization. Rural African American farmers saw traditional farming as a part of their church life. Many people rode to church in wagons and on mules and horses. These were seen on church grounds during worship services. They burned in the stove the wood which was sawed or chopped by members. They drank water at church from a well or pump on the church ground or from the home of a nearby member. Usually the benches in the church were made by members. Grass and weeds on the church yard were cut by members with hoes, sickles, or swingblades. The people generally erected their own church buildings from materials they bought or made. It is easy to perceive that self-determination is not easily realized among African American church farmers with changes in agricultural technology, economy, urbanization, mobility, and modern life.

Insecurity is and has been overwhelming to the African American rural congregations. Such questions inevitably arise: How do we survive? Should we let our churches go? Should our churches merge with stronger and larger churches? Will the members be willing to attend church in another town? Can we get resident pastors if we do not have the money to support them? Can we call upon our mission boards to provide us with necessary financial means to support pastors? Why can't we have lay ministers within the congregations to carry on ministerial acts and responsibilities? In many cases, people conclude, "We just don't know what to do." Some say, "We just won't attend church but will have church at home." Others even say, "We'll join a church of another denomination nearby; we're going to somebody's church to worship God."

When African American churchmen assert, "We teach and preach the Word of God in its truth and purity, and we administer the Sacraments according to their divine institution by Christ," outside observers may ask, "Why are these people so insecure? They have the Word of God. They are Christians saved by God's grace for Christ's sake through faith. They should cling to God's Word more, believe more, pray more, and get out there and 'hit the bushes' for more people. After all, the Lord helps those who help themselves." But asserting the preceding does not rescue the rural church victims from their dilemma. It is obvious that many African American Christians in rural areas experience a certain amount of insecurity. In other words, they lack the resources to satisfy their needs sufficiently.

Worthlessness is envisioned by a number of African American churches in rural areas. Since they do not have the resources—a pastor, money, a "respectable" membership, an "acceptable" church support, and participatory church attendance—members tend to feel a sense of worthlessness. Such questions arise: "Why should we try to continue these small rural churches? We have no full-time pastors. A lot of the members live somewhere else; there is little money being given; people do not like to go to a church where there is hardly anybody in attendance. All the youth are gone; parents don't bring their children to Sunday school like they should; that leaves only a few oldsters around here to die."

The feeling of worthlessness was common even in biblical times. After the draught of fishes, Simon Peter said to Jesus, "Depart from me; for I am a sinful man, O Lord" (Luke

5:8). During Isaiah's vision in the temple, he confessed, "Woe is me! for I am undone; because I am a man of unclean lips, and I dwell in the midst of a people of unclean lips" (Isaiah 6:5). The Roman centurion asserted to Jesus, "I am not worthy that thou shouldest enter under my roof" (Luke 7:6). People who feel worthless need the Lord's gracious help. Moreover, other Christians need to reach out to such people in active love and uplifting service as Christ's servants.

Lovelessness is a sensitivity that is not hidden among rural church people. They sincerely believe that they are embraced with God's love, for "God is love" (1 John 4:8). God's love is all-inclusive to all people—urban and rural or whomever and wherever they are. "For God so loved the world, that He gave His only begotten Son, that whosoever believeth in Him should not perish, but have everlasting life" (John 3:16).

It appears that the love rural church people miss the most is not God's love, not the love of other Christians in the world, but love of members of their own churches and their own families who have gone away. Some examples are young men and women who have gone into the armed services or to college; middle-aged men and women who have left the farm for job opportunities; men and women who have migrated to urban communities for a better life. Love of people seems to falter and fall apart when loved ones must part by a force over which victims have no control. Family members forced to part from other family members, neighbors compelled to separate from their much-appreciated neighbors; long-time acquaintances in the community suffer from a chasm of long distance by persons who must move on to other places.

Many rural churches seem to be left with two options: *conquer or escape.* There is the possibility that church members can hold on to their churches by fighting "the good fight of faith" and against all odds remain alive and succeed. Or church members look for a way of escape such as leaving, transferring their membership elsewhere, amalgamating their congregations with a larger and stronger congregation, or merging a number of smaller churches into one congregation.

A glowing example of rural churches holding on or letting go is seen in Alabama. A study was made by the Rev. Thomas Noon of black Lutheran congregations in the Black Belt area. The study indicates that there were 32 African American Lutheran congregations during the first half of this century. Of the 32 churches and mission stations, 25 or more were in rural areas. Some of these rural churches and/or mission stations collapsed; others merged into one central congregation; a minimal four congregations remain in existence.

According to Dr. Richard C. Dickinson, there were rural, black churches also in other states as follows:

North Carolina 6

Virginia 1

Louisiana 1

Total 8

Of these eight, only three still survive.

SUGGESTED DIRECTIVES FOR RURAL CHURCHES

Several suggestions are given below to be considered to serve as directives to African American rural churches. Three practical implications are indicated by the Rev. Guido Merkens that can be applied to rural churches: prayer, celebration, and caring.

1. **Prayer.** Spend lengthy periods of time in fervent prayer, communing reverently and sincerely with the heav-

enly Father. Ask for a bountiful measure of the Holy Spirit to provide "power from on high" (Luke 24:49). Pray in faith, believing whatsoever we ask the Father in Jesus' name, He will give it to us (John 16:23).

2. **Celebration.** Church worship should be a joyful and meaningful celebration. The worship service should be one in which the worshipers can participate and relate to their personal concerns and should be meaningful and satisfying. Above all, worship should be grounded in the Word of God and the Sacraments, utilized as vital truths through which the Holy Spirit works. Jesus affirms, "But the hour cometh, and now is, when the true worshippers shall worship the Father in spirit and truth: for the Father seeketh such to worship Him" (John 4:23).

3. **Caring.** The rural church should consist of caring people, including the members as well as the pastor. The caring should be extended into the community as well as in the congregation. Caring for people should include the following:

Visiting the sick

Comforting mourners

Strengthening the weak

Offering direction to the straying

Speaking Christ's forgiveness to sinners

Proclaiming the Gospel to the lost

Pointing the dying to heaven

Other directives are based on happenings at Pilgrim Lutheran Church, Freedom, Missouri, where the writer has rendered pastoral services for the past 20 years. Although the parishioners and community people are of Germanic ancestry, most of the activities that take place in Freedom can be made applicable in other rural parishes regardless of the nationality or ethnic identity of members. Hence, the writer presents the additional items below for consideration, adoption, and usage.

4. The rural church may secure a worker priest—an ordained minister who is engaged in an avocation or another job, or it may make arrangement to attain a retired pastor. The writer served Pilgrim Lutheran Church, Freedom, as a worker-priest for 11 years while he was a professor at Lincoln University in Jefferson City, Missouri. Since his retirement from Lincoln eight years ago, he has continued to serve Pilgrim Congregation as its pastor.

5. The rural church may be able to engage the service of a licensed lay minister. Such a person may be secured upon the approval of the colloquy committee of the parent church body.

A neighboring church, Shepherd of the Hills Lutheran Church in Hermann, Missouri, had a lay minister for a number of years until his retirement. The writer was one of the pastors to give pastoral leadership to that mission congregation prior to the appointment of the lay minister.

6. A strong vacation Bible school for preschool children through high school seniors may prove vital. Some of the high school students can serve as helpers for odd jobs and as teacher assistants. For the 1995 one-week vacation Bible school at Pilgrim Church, there was an enrollment of over 100 participants. A very capable lay director did an excellent organizational and administrative job with help of a staff of 22 persons. The director and staff members used their cars and vans to pick up and return students to their homes. Some of the benefits of the vacation Bible school are teaching the Word of God, rendering a service to the children and parents in our congregation and the wider community, opening the door to gain new members, and enhancing the church's spiritual image and its servant role to the whole community.

7. The house-mission approach has proved very effective in the wider Freedom community. Families were identified that were not active church members. Upon contacting some of these families and getting their permission, the pastor established biblical-instruction meetings in their homes. Certain Sundays were designated for reception of new members by confirmation and Baptism together with membership transfers. The results in 1993 were 30 new members, mostly new converts.

8. The observance of a church anniversary can prove beneficial. Pilgrim Church celebrated its 125th anniversary on August 8, 1993. It was meaningful and impressive to members, the small-town community people, and former baptized and confirmed members. Two ladies and the pastor planned the celebration with the committed support of the voters' assembly, ladies aid, altar guild, youth group, the adult and youth choirs, the Sunday school, and individual faithful members. There was a festive service followed by a luncheon, and ending with an outdoor informal service. The preacher for both services was the honorary Lutheran Hour speaker, The Rev. Dr. Oswald Hoffmann. A guest trio sang songs outdoors to bridge the gap between the luncheon at 11:30 A.M. and the outdoor service at 1:00 P.M. The anniversary booklet contained the worship service items, a history of the church, and photographs of pastors having served the church. Also available in the "Liescheidt Schoolhouse" was a display of pictures of former buildings, confirmation classes, and others. A closed-circuit TV showed the service on the lawn to the overflow crowd during the inside service of the morning and inside the church during the outdoor afternoon service for persons who desired to be on the inside. Publicity regarding the services was given special attention in the local newspapers, to local churches, and by invitations to neighbors and out-of-town friends and/or relatives.

9. Another directive for rural parish work is rural culture. As a professional adult educator for 28 years, a rural pastor for 20 years, and a growing-up boy in the country for 20 years, the writer is in accord with Rev. Eldor Meyer and Wendell Berry that there is a local rural culture briefly deliberated on below.

In general and at the same time in particular, rural culture is to be considered a part of working effectively with people in rural churches. While they feel a part of the overall American culture and have respect for their parent church bodies, they are fervent adherents to their own rural culture. Example: Rural people will use their rights to vote in a national election, follow national happenings and news. But they seem to appreciate associating and knowing their local leaders with whom they are familiar. Their local newspaper and other media are very dear to them. Many of their decisions and much of their overt behavior reflect what is going on in their community. Rural church people appreciate an abiding affiliation with a parent church body, but they have their own way of doing certain things and are resistant to change that will infringe upon the satisfaction of their way of life. Handed down by foreparents are the values, customs, habits, traditions, rules, and mores. These are deeply rooted in strengthening rural people in the philosophy of common sense and experiencing the Maslowian concept in satisfying their needs—physiological, safety, loving and belonging, esteem and self-actualization.

10. A final directive for thought and usage is publicity. Good publicity and genuine public relations can have magnetic effects toward being an alive and well church. Such publicity should include the newspaper, radio, and television. Church bulletins, letters, and fliers can prove effective in keeping the church before the public eye and serving as a means of sharing the Gospel. Communication by tele-

phone and in person are some of the best means of publicity. The central ideal of publicity is public relations: relating the church and its functions to the various publics. This includes an attractive outside bulletin board with pertinent information and a neat and caring appearance of the church's property. Moreover, church members should have visible representation at community affairs such as dinners, suppers, art shows, concerts, graduation exercises, and more. Uppermost is for church members to behave and enact "They'll know we are Christians by our love."

SOME CONCLUDING THOUGHTS

Rural people are creatures of God in need of a spiritual relationship with God. A stable and active rural congregation helps to nurture that relationship. Rural Christians are a part of the larger church, the body of Christ, and the church is called upon to serve all people.

We are witnessing a reverse migration from large urban areas to less congested and slower-paced communities. People are seeking seemingly safer, cleaner, more congenial communities, ones in which there is familylike support. Some return to rural areas to claim a family's inheritance; others seek out rural communities as appropriate places for retirement; still others go for reasons of health. The rural church plays a role in healing individuals and groups of people and enhancing wholeness and cohesiveness in the rural community.

Rural churches provide an opportunity for creative leadership; they require a new look at the ministry and substantial lay involvement. These churches call for flexibility and innovation in worship services, some of which may need to be tailored to specific congregations. Ministers working in rural areas need a certain liberty to act independently; congregations need not always be involved in ministers' activities. Modern circuit riders may prove useful in carrying on the mission and ministry in small rural churches and communities.

We must consider innovative directives and/or implications for the future if rural churches are to be viable, vital, and productive. The church needs a holistic, evangelistic approach in order to get the job done. There are some laid-back behaviors that need to be examined and changed in order for the church to be effective in gaining and keeping all sorts and conditions of people for Christ's kingdom on earth.

Procedures for gaining and retaining new members that have proven to be effective for the writer are below:

1. Identify family with unchurched persons in it.
2. Make appointment to meet with family.
3. Pray for God's blessings before meeting with family.
4. Make visit with family at convenient time.
5. Confront family members with the Christian religion.
6. Get commitment for becoming active Christians and church members; end meeting with prayer for the Holy Spirit's blessing.
7. Pursue flexible home instructions in Christian teachings.
8. Set date immediately for reception into church membership.
9. Receive into membership on date set by appropriate rites: Baptism, confirmation, or profession of faith.
10. Establish flexible procedures for welcoming and retaining new members.

If the rural church is to reach out in its mission and ministry, it is vitally important that church members show Christ's care, love, and concern for people in the community as well as in their congregations. For example, if there is a death in a family in the community, the church should show some caring concern such as sending sympathy cards, phone calls offering services, visiting informally, going to funeral homes, or even giving some kind of visible gift such as a fruit basket or flower plant. Another example would be if there is sickness in a community home, the church should do one or more things: Send get-well cards, make impromptu calls to say they've heard about it, or present a visible gift such as food the patient may like. Uppermost in church people's minds ought to be 1 Timothy 2:3-4: "God our Savior ... will have all men to be saved, and to come unto the knowledge of the truth."

Bibliography

Barrett, Lois. *Building the House Church*. Scottsdale, PA: Herald Press, 1986.

Biegner, Paul. *Thriving, Beyond Surviving*. Burnsville, MN: Rural Small Town Church Conference of the Minnesota South District of The Lutheran Church—Missouri Synod, 1993. Videocassette.

Dickinson, Richard C. *Roses and Thorns*. St. Louis: Concordia Publishing House, 1977.

Huth, Walter A. *The Challenge of Rural Ministry*. St. Louis: Concordia Publishing House, n.d. audiocassette.

Krueger, Carl. *Reaching People in a Rural Setting*. St. Louis: Concordia Seminary, n.d. audiocassette.

Maslow, Abraham. *Motivation and Personality*. New York: Harper and Row, 1970.

Merkens, Guido. *Conversations at Presidium Meetings, 1986–1989*. St. Louis: The Lutheran Church—Missouri Synod, n.d.

CHURCH WORK IN RURAL COMMUNITIES

Meyer, Eldor. *Joys, Blessings and Benefits of Rural Ministry.* Burnsville, MN: Rural Small Town Church Conference of the Minnesota South District of The Lutheran Church—Missouri Synod, 1993. Videocassette.

Noon, Thomas. *A Tourguide of Former Black Lutheran Synodical Conference/Lutheran Church—Missouri Synod Congregations in the Black Belt Area.* Birmingham: Alabama Black Lutheran Heritage Association, St. Paul Lutheran Church, 1991.

One Hundred Twenty-Five Years of Blessings. Freedom, Missouri: Pilgrim Lutheran Church, 1993.

SUGGESTED ADDITIONAL READINGS

Berry, Wendell. *What Are People For?* San Francisco: North Point Press, 1990.

Schaller, Lyle. *The Small Church Is Different.* Nashville: Abingdon Press, 1982.

Smith, Rockwell C. *Rural Ministry and the Changing Community.* Nashville: Abingdon Press, 1971.

Zunkel, C. Wayne. *Growing the Small Church.* Elgin, IL: David C. Cook, 1982.

6

African American Families and the Church

Phillip A. Campbell

Many black families are discontinuing, breaking up, living in chaotic relationships, or to view the picture objectively, "withering away." While the causes have evolved historically, the response is even more historical: rooted in God's Word. For numerous black families, the male/female relationships are practiced contrary to scripture. The church can and should teach God's commands for family structure. This also implies that black males need socialization training from childhood throughout life.

AN HISTORICAL PERSPECTIVE

The family is the basic component of every society. It is where the primary socialization process takes place. It is the "nursery of human nature." The importance of the family in the moral and religious development of children has been recognized since the beginning of the human race. Within Judaism, Christianity, and most religions of the world, the institution of the family has been safeguarded jealously.

In both the Old and New Testaments, the relationship between God and human beings is often described in terms drawn imaginarily from the family. The family is considered to be the natural human institution that most fully embodies the ideas of true community among men and most fully symbolizes the relationship between God and believers in the community of faith.

The family today is undergoing deep-rooted changes, especially in the Western and industrialized nations of the world. The family no longer exercises its authoritarian controls and codes of morality. It is no longer bound together by economic necessity. The patriarchal mode is under attack. The family is withering away through neglect of its members to face up seriously to the question of "What ought a family to be?" This general withering of the family is even more apparent and devastating on the African American family than on white families. The Population Profile for 1993 (Bureau of the Census) states that during the mid-1980s, discontinuance was more likely for black than for white families (12 percent compared with 7 percent). About one in every 12 two-parent families existing at the start of any two-year period in the mid 1980s no longer existed two years later. The family would join a different household that already existed, or there was separation of husband and wife. Sometimes one died. But whatever the cause, a new single-parent family was the result. And there is greater likelihood that a two-parent family will break-up if the father is not employed. Add to this the large numbers of poor families, teenage parents, and drugs, and we see human conditions which accelerate the withering.

If the traditional family is experiencing serious changes, the church, the carrier of traditions, is undergoing similar transitions, because the families make the church.

111

The question can be raised, "What ought a church be to the family seeking what it ought to be?"

The black church, like the African American family, is modeled after the prevailing dominant white culture, basically because of the lack of other models and the conditions of slavery. Unlike its white counterpart, the black church goes beyond the ideological and theological emphasis of white churches to an ideology and theology of practice, rooted in the Christian faith. The black church offered and offers a religion for oppressed people. It gives them the strength to continue to exist and survive in a society of oppression, segregation, and discrimination.

The writer is in agreement with Joseph Hough, that the church has always played a very important role in the life of the African American community. The church was the only kind of social organization available to blacks and the only place where, on occasion, they could come out of the hostile world, be strengthened from their togetherness, and find a base of new hope.

To summarize, throughout all centuries the institution of the family has been preserved. A vital force in this historical preservation is the Christian church. The black church has been fundamentally significant in the lives of black families. With these facts in mind, we now summarize three related concerns which have surfaced in this section: 1) Families are withering away, breaking up, discontinuing at a faster rate among black families than among other populations in the United States. 2) The question is raised, what ought a church be to the family seeking what it ought to be? 3) The black church offers strength and encouragement to individuals and families in a society of oppression.

A family is as strong and as stable as those elements and forces that promote and encourage its stability. The Christian church is among those strong, vital forces. When the church ceases to serve those enhancing features, the family begins to disintegrate, and so does society. The church ought to be that force for God which is ever aware of societal changes. It ought to encourage those basic Christian values which are necessary for survival and help to guide the family through the change, not fearful of suggesting alternatives and options to make family life more meaningful.

MALE-FEMALE ROLES AND RELATIONSHIPS

At the forefront of the withering family in America and even more so for African American families is the male-female relationship. On this crucial issue hinges the theoretical solutions to many other African American problems.

Because of technological advances, women rights, and usurping of traditionally-assigned male-female roles of western society, the relationship between men and women has become strained, as old values are discarded and ever-changing new ones are being adopted without being completely verified. Such new values leave numerous blacks single or divorced and searching for answers and solutions to their problems.

While attempting to find solutions to those undefined problems amidst values and roles, relationships between many African American men and women have become strained, leading to anger which directly affects many black families. The church as an institution has just begun to deal seriously with the enmity that exists between some black men and women as its clergy has become skilled in disciplines other than theology.

If the withering of the African American family is to be slowed or stopped, the issue of black male-female relationships must be addressed by the church, which is the only institution with the legitimacy and the authority in the black community to aid in the resolution of this critical conflict affecting the family.

The family is no longer a rural, agrarian economic unit. Because of technology, women no longer stay at home to make bread and take care of the babies, while the men work in the fields. Often out of economic necessity and due to the advent of computers and high technology, women are capable of nearly all the jobs men are. Physical strength, in terms of earning power, no longer separates the sexes. Within the family, God did set forth a structural hierarchy of authority with the man at the head of that structure. References are found throughout the Holy Scripture: Genesis 2; Mark 10; Matthew 19; Romans 7; 1 Timothy 3; which are also reinforced in most marriage vows, based on the divine truth that God is the head of His creation and Jesus Christ is the head of the church. Destroy or pervert that structure, and we have chaos and confusion, expressly deterioration of male-female relationships and a breakdown of the family.

Today that ideal, God-modeled structure is being perverted in our western society. We all recognize that the western democratic economy operates on capitalism. The more money one possesses, the more authority (power) one is able to exercise. That's not the way it ought to be, but that's the way it is.

If the money-equals-power standard is applied to the original family structure, a perversion of the hierarchy of authority is inevitable. The family members who make the most money are often the ones who exercise the most power in families or in male-female relationships. In terms of economic survival in today's family, a man is not necessary. Women are doing as well and often better financially than their male counterparts. Since economic earning power seems to be a prime indicator of authority, male authority, which is his prime role in the hierarchial structure, is diminished or not recognized—which is a perversion of the original ideal God-model.

A man is the "stand-in." That is the structure in many cases. He should be the authority figure in the family. The woman is the help-mate, she is the supportive one and takes the man's place only when he is absent or incapacitated in some way. The male is the recognized authority figure in nearly every society on the face of the earth. The failure to recognize such is both foolish and dangerous.

The most volatile and explosive elements in our society today are young men—even more so, angry young African American males. The underlying cause of the withering and deterioration of the family appears to be the lack of clarification of male-female roles, which is often interpreted by many males as the loss of authority or power.

An example of a recognized male role may be seen in an African boy taken into the forest at a certain age and being indoctrinated for four moons into the ways of manhood and circumcised. When he returns to his village, his authority is recognized. His role in the family and the community is clear.

Today we have no clear-cut rites of passage, and the male role, according to God's hierarchial structure, is being challenged or not recognized. We are paying horrible prices. It is not the female that we fear when we walk the streets. It is not the female who perpetuates mugging, robberies, rapes, and most murders. It is not the female who so often commits the ultimate act of human frustration: suicide. Such pathological patterns have a tendency to come from families in which male authority is not present or not recognized. To move the family from such pathological patterns, it is desired that there be more giving, sharing, and loving.

THE CHURCH AND GENDER ROLE CLARIFICATION

Before turning our thinking to concerns for the future, this section is beginning with some additional background information regarding the father-authority-figure role. This is a concern because of deep-rooted, oppressed thinking that should be understood in order for churches to plan and guide meaningful change that is precise and effective.

A family is not a democratic institution, though it may practice democracy. There is within the family a designated power structure given by God Himself. And even when that authority cannot be exercised, it must at least be recognized.

The African American family in the United States emerged from that peculiar institution called slavery. It adopted the family pattern of the prevailing culture. The prevailing family pattern was that of a patriarchal (father) role. Such a model has scriptural and traditional support and fulfills the hierarchial structure as the male being the authority figure in the family.

The role of the patriarch is to provide the family with the necessary material sustenance for survival, to protect and defend it from destructive internal and external forces, and to give it a general sense of direction and goals.

The African American family under the peculiar institution of slavery had no such protection, because the father in the family had no rights or privileges separate from those of his master. The black woman, out of necessity, often became head of the household, giving rise to matriarchy (mother rule), so prevalent among black families today. It should be noted that the black woman didn't become head of the family because she wanted to or because she thought it right or even equal rights. She

116

became head because to her master she was "less expendable" than the black male.

The black woman was an economic asset by her gender. She could birth more slaves. She was a controlling asset by her effective socialization of family members to the will of the master. She could raise her children to be good slaves. She was a pleasure asset by her gender. Because she had no protection, she could be used as a sex object at the discretion of her master. Though the black woman's sacrificial actions are not looked upon today as great virtue, they were very positive and necessary for family survival. Some wise individual once said, "Be not so quick to judge from the height one has risen, but judge from the depth which one has climbed."

The "colored church" was one of the few places wherein the black male could exercise patriarchal authority and the female could receive necessary support. The family survived because the woman survived and because the church survived. It was and ought to be an inter-dependant cycle.

The psalmist has written, "God setteth the solitary in families: He bringeth out those which are bound with chains" (Ps. 68:6). We have all been placed in families—individual families, extended families, and those who don't know that they have families or think that they don't have families. Through the sacrifice of His Son, Jesus, God has made it possible for believers to belong to the family of God. Life is more meaningful in the context of a family. In spite of any historical, intellectual, or spiritual crises, the counteracting power of preserving and healing has been the family.

The family has survived. We the living can testify to that survival. It has been a shaky survival, and the worse may yet be forthcoming. The African American family today finds itself dwelling under the pervasion of capitalism, emulating the family patterns of the dominant culture, living with the residual effects of that peculiar institution called slavery, and out of necessity practicing matriarchy. This is not the model that God has given us, but one can well understand the role confusion and the male-female conflict.

As previously stated, the family is not a democratic institution, though it may practice democracy. It is not a 50–50 venture whereby role functions are agreed and voted upon. Necessary role functions must be performed by those members of the family who have the ability. Such role functions are irrespective of gender. Greater will be the burden of responsibility on that member who has the most abilities. Jesus said, "For unto whomsoever much is given, of him shall much be required: and to whom men have committed much, of him they will ask the more" (Luke 12:48). That burden of responsibility may fall upon a father, a mother, a son, a daughter, or even a grandparent.

If I were a bold person, I would set forth a general role clarification for men and women in today's society. I would say that African American men must be recognized as the authority figure in the family, and they must accept the joy and the painful burden of responsibility. The failure to recognize and accept such is an invitation to disaster. If I were even more bold, I would suggest that the female role in the family should be that of a socializing agent. To fail in that area is even more dangerous. A man may have all the authority in the world, but if he has not been socialized in the proper use of power, he can become a tyrant, destructive to self, family, and society. The role of an authority figure is given or taken, but the *proper* use of authority is learned.

As aforestated, when the home fails, so does society. While government and politics are often blamed for many of the conditions with family, we must remember that directly or indirectly, the home is the strong force behind both the evil and the good in society. All churches in the past and present are in some way affected by all conditions of people and furthermore are in the position to give some relief. The same inherently continues to the future. Conditions of people in society include rich or poor, elderly or young, single or married, parents or nonparents, disabled or not disabled, literate or illiterate, employed or unemployed, dysfunctional families or functional families, and other and any combinations of these. To this list we can add the dilemmas posed by drugs, AIDS, abortions, teenage heads of families, welfare problems, and as already stated, any combinations.

Poverty is one of the observable characteristics associated with most of the undesirable family structures, and the same is true for black families. Poor, two-parent families are more likely to break up than nonpoor ones. Many poor, single mothers who recently formed their own households came from households where they were already poor. According to Poverty in the United States: 1992, Bureau of the Census, 33.3 percent of blacks were poor. However, the majority of poor persons in the United States were white. Children under six years of age have been particularly vulnerable to poverty. In 1992, black children represented 16.3 percent of all children under six years of age but represented 34.6 percent of the poor children in this age group. Blacks in general constituted 12.6 percent of all persons but 28.8 percent of the poor. The writer concurs with Lincoln and Mamiya that, since economic values are both primary and predominant in American society and are commonly used to determine social relations and social status, the most severe forms of racial discrimination against black people have been economic in nature. Thus, the economic poverty is apparent.

When persons in poverty are not taught Christian principles through the church, those persons can become victims of increased exploitation of the roles of father and mother and inevitably accelerate the family withering away. For the family to be preserved, those principles must also be learned. When children, poor or rich, are socialized in Christianity, there should be less proneness towards drugs and other self-inflicted ills. A woman may have all the rights in the world, but if she fails to socialize her offspring, she may live to regret that she ever birthed sons and daughters into the world. Fathers and mothers are to be assisted by the church to teach Christian living. The poor and the rich can live in Christian, God-pleasing families. The numbers of poor blacks surfaced above help to show that many persons are in society who, without the church's intervention, are hazardous to themselves and others. They need to learn of Christ, their Savior, to understand and practice the Christian way of life. When the family fails, so does society. As is the mother, so often will be the daughter. As is the father, so often will be the son. We are not born with Christian principles; they are taught and learned. If we build our families on the principles of God's Word, they will have a sure foundation for remaining firm, strong, purposeful, and spiritually functional.

Bibliography

Anschen, Ruth. "The Family—Its Function and Destiny." *Religious Quotes,* 1949.

Clark, Kenneth, and Talcott Parson. *The Negro American.* Boston: Beacon Press, 1966.

Hough, Joseph, Jr. *Black Power and White Protestants.* Oxford, England: Oxford Press, 1968.

Lincoln, C. Eric, and Lawrence Mamiya. *The Black Church and the African American Experience.* Durham, N.C.: Duke University Press, 1990.

"Mistakes Black Men Make in Relating to Black Women." *Ebony,* 1975.

Population Profile of the United States: U. S. Bureau of the Census, Current Population Reports. Washington, D. C.: U. S. Government Printing Press, 1993.

Poverty in the United States: U. S. Bureau of the Census, Current Population Reports. Washington, D. C.: U. S. Government Printing Office, 1993.

SUGGESTED ADDITIONAL READINGS

Blackburn, Bill, and Deanna Mattingly Blackburn. *Caring in Times of Family Crisis.* Nashville: Abingdon Press, 1987.

Campbell, Phillip. *Future Family: Ethnic Directions for Black Americans and Others.* Winona, MN: Appollo Books, 1983.

Christensen, Larry. *The Christian Family.* Minneapolis: Bethany Fellowship, Inc., 1970.

Hunt, Richard. "Working with Single Parents." In *Handbook on Religious Education,* edited by Nancy T. Foltz. Birmingham, AL: Religious Education Press, 1986.

Lidums, Susan B. *Church Family Ministry; Changing Loneliness to Fellowship in the Church.* St. Louis: Concordia Publishing House, 1985.

7

The Future of Black Ministry in the Church

Bryant E. Clancy, Jr.

Stand at the crossroads and look; ask for the ancient paths, ask where the good way is, and walk in it, and you will find rest for your souls. Jeremiah 6:16 NIV

A PILGRIM JOURNEY

My mother is a second generation Lutheran. Although she was born and reared in the Lutheran church, she knew and sang many of the spirituals in the morning as she prepared the family breakfast. The spiritual "I Want Jesus to Walk with Me" was most dear to her. The writer believes it was her morning prayer, because she sang it with so much feeling. The words are

> *I want Jesus to walk with me;*
> *I want Jesus to walk with me;*
> *All along my pilgrim journey,*
> *Lord, I want Jesus to walk with me.*
>
> *In my trials, Lord, walk with me;*
> *In my trials, Lord, walk with me;*

When my heart is almost breaking,
Lord, I want Jesus to walk with me.

When I'm in trouble, Lord walk with me;
When I'm in trouble, Lord walk with me;
When my head is bowed in sorrow,
Lord, I want Jesus to walk with me.

"Pilgrim Journey," conceptualized by the writer, is the vantage point from which this chapter is written. It deals with circumstances, events, emotions, and being a person on a journey through time. Congregations form the context for the pilgrim journey. In this chapter, Lutheranism is the context, and faith in the Lord Jesus Christ is the major focal point for the pilgrim. This makes the journey spiritual. African American Lutheran history will be described in broad strokes rather than the citation of individuals and events. The present will be seen through the energy being exerted to focus the vision, plans, goals, and steps to achieve specific outcomes. The future will serve this chapter like the Star of Bethlehem, by which people are guided to the manger of our Savior Jesus Christ.

Black ministry is a 118-year-old pilgrim in The Lutheran Church—Missouri Synod. This journey has had many beginning points from the late 1800s to the present. Louisiana is a door through which 2,059 souls, in 14 congregations, began the journey in response to the Good News of Jesus as Savior.

Alabama was the beginning point on the journey for 34 congregations and 2,684 pilgrims in 1916. Until this day, pilgrims have been coming forth singing that song, "Lord, I want Jesus to come and walk with me."

Georgia, South Carolina, North Carolina, Virginia, Washington, D. C., and Maryland provided other entrances to the journey for 37 congregations in which 3,263 pilgrims took up the song cited above. A large number continue to sing the song.

New York and Philadelphia are other ports of entrance for 23 congregations and 2,584 pilgrims. These ports continue to provide a rich pilgrim harvest.

The Lord opened doors in the west—Ohio, Missouri, Illinois, Michigan, and California. Eighteen congregations appeared with 3,379 pilgrims. Those congregations continue with noteworthy visibility.

This pilgrim journey gathers from all over the nations, from most of the 50 states and from 25 of the 35 districts of The Lutheran Church—Missouri Synod. In every place and in each congregations it seems the plea is heard, "Lord, I want Jesus to walk with me. All along this pilgrim journey, Lord, I want Jesus to walk with me."

THE PILGRIM JOURNEY AS A WORK OF GOD

The pilgrim journey is a work of God through people of faith, energized by the Gospel, which is the "power of God for the salvation of everyone who believes" (Rom. 1:16 NIV). With and through this Gospel of our Lord Jesus Christ, whom God has made to be sin for us, God raised up leaders with extraordinary vision and missionary zeal for ministry among the colored or Negroes from slavery time to mid-1960, blacks or Afro-Americans from mid-1960 to mid-1980, and blacks or African Americans from mid-1980s to the present. God equipped these leaders with His Word and Sacraments, faith deeply rooted in the promises of God, genuine love for people, and unrelenting commitment to share Christ with them. Moreover, the Holy Spirit moved these dedicated leaders to teach the Scriptures in their hearing, to worship, and to serve with them as the people of God. They went forth as missionaries on the pilgrim journey.

In the 1700s, the Lutheran Salzburgers brought Lutheranism to Georgia (Dickinson, 20). The unusualness of their faith is that they not only actively sought to convert slaves, but as part of that effort they deliberately taught some of their slaves to read and write (Johnson, 63).

In the mid-1800s, before the birth of the Evangelical Lutheran Synodical Conference, St. John Lutheran Church, Charleston, South Carolina, exemplified an authentic strategy for ministry. It was a congregation in which master, slave, and freedman worshiped and reached out to others. In this unique congregation were 200 black communicants and a 150-member Sunday school. Jeff Johnson lists seven distinguishing factors about the congregation.

> (1) Blacks had their own worship services, [at which they] "sing and pray, read the Scriptures, and exhort each other to the faithful discharge of their Christian duties." (2) Blacks had their own leaders in the church who were both slave and free. ... (3) Blacks had their own Sunday school and their own Sunday school staff. (4) Black leaders were usually expected to settle disciplinary problems that arose among communicants. (5) Black teams visited the sick. (6) Blacks conducted their own burial services. (7) Blacks had their own ... burial society that had its own cemetery ... (Johnson, 118; point 1 quotes R. M. Bost, "The Reverend John Bachman and the Development of Southern Lutherans." A dissertation, Yale University, 1963, 389, footnote 34).

With eyes clearly focused on the future, Rev. Stephen A. Mealy, president of the South Carolina Synod, cast the vision: "It is my deliberate impression that if rightly approached [hundreds of Negroes] would become worthy members of our communion" (Johnson, 118, quoting *Extracts of the Minutes of the Fourteenth Synod and*

Ministerium of South Carolina and Adjacent States, Charleston, 1837, 38).

In 1872, God caused the four synods to come together in the Evangelical Lutheran Synodical Conference around these purposes:

> To give outward expression to the unity of spirit existing among the constituent synods; to encourage and strengthen one another in faith and confession; to further unity in doctrine and practice and to remove whatever might threaten to disturb this unity; to co-operate in matters of mutual interest; to strive for true unity in doctrine and practice among Lutheran church bodies (*Synodical Conference Proceedings* [hereafter *Proceedings*], vol. 33-39, 127).

At the convention on July 18-24, 1877, Rev. H.A. Preus brought before the convention the resolution "to begin mission work among the colored people of the United States" (Mueller, 24). With that resolve The Lutheran Church—Missouri Synod, the Norwegian Synod of the American Lutheran Church, the Slovak Evangelical Lutheran Synod, and the Wisconsin, Minnesota, Michigan Synods began and exercised "control [over] the Colored Missions" (Mueller, 22-23).

Can it be that God brought these synods together to receive the request for help from his servant, Rosa Young? Is it possible that God convened these synods to send them forth with the Great Commission mandate to open the Lutheran door to slaves and their heirs? What divine significance from the perspective of black Americans shall we attach to the formation of the Evangelical Lutheran Synodical Conference and the resolution brought by H.A. Preus? Rosa Young answers the questions in this manner:

> The coming of the Lutheran church into Alabama was providential. God only used me and the Rosebud school as instruments to place this church in the Black

THE FUTURE OF BLACK MINISTRY IN THE CHURCH

Belt and to lead us poor sinners out of spiritual darkness into light. ... God, who is able to do all things, could have used any of the other sources to whom I had so earnestly appealed for help to sustain the school, but He caused every other source to which I applied to refuse me help until I had applied to the right source. ... It was a direct answer to my prayer (Young, 110).

The answer to the question "Why are you a Black Lutheran?" is, "By the design and providence of God." The promise of God is that His Word "will not return ... empty, but will accomplish what I desire and achieve the purpose for which I sent it" (Isaiah 55:11 NIV). The 50,000 Black Lutherans now and the 100,000 anticipated in the new century are visualized in this design. The work of Rosa Young demonstrates how this new century goal can be accomplished. Rev. Thomas Noon, writing about the history of the Southern District and Dr. Young's work, said,

By the end of 1916 some seven additional missions had been spawned. St. Paul's, Oak Hill, Alabama, four miles southeast of Rosebud, was begun through the impetus of confirmand James McBride, who lived in the vicinity. St. Andrews, Vredenburgh, Alabama, fifteen miles southwest in Monroe County, was initiated by confirmands Mary and Sarah McCants, who boarded in Rosebud but lived in Vredenburgh. Alex Etheridge, who lived in Possum Bend, Alabama, heard of the Lutherans and went to Rosebud to listen to the preaching and teaching which went on during some nights. He encouraged a mission in his community some five miles east of Camden (*Proceedings,* vol. 33–39, 52).

Rev. Noon reported many stories like this.

The two attempts to do on a national level what was practiced at St. John Lutheran Church, Charleston, South Carolina, were unsuccessful. The first effort consisted in organizing the Alpha Synod in North Carolina under the leadership of D. J. Koontz in 1890. The second attempt came with the 1944 "Proposed Constitution for the Organization of the Negro Congregations of the Evangelical Lutheran Synodical Conference of North America, as a recommendation of the Committee on the Survey of Negro Missions" (*Proceedings,* vol. 43–46, 24). The report around the discussion of this proposal received a "yes, but not now" reply. It did not matter that this ministry had a 65-year development history. It was true that experience had taught the wisdom of indigenous leadership, "but the time was not ripe for it." The knowledge that Negroes should have voice, a vote, and leadership was there, but there was no courage to make it so. Therefore, the Missionary Board was recognized to allow for a General Board. The membership criteria provided for a nine-member board with one Negro member.

The 46th Convention of the Evangelical Lutheran Synodical Conference resolved to encourage synodical congregations to become affiliated with the district in which they were located. On their part, districts accepted the challenge of receiving these congregations into their care and ministry. However, nowhere does one read of this ministry receiving top priority or the embrace of empowering missionary policies. The Synodical Conference Congregations integration into districts took place over a 16-year period. The "whereases" to a resolution before the 1961 recessed Forty-Sixth Convention of the Synodical Conference referenced a progress report given by the Board of Directors of The Lutheran Church—Missouri Synod.

> Whereas, In accordance with the recommendations by the Synodical Conference Convention in 1946 individual Districts of The Lutheran Church—Missouri Synod have in every instance but one accepted the responsi-

bility for the mission work among the Negroes in their respective districts; and

Whereas, The one remaining district, namely, the Southern District, has offered and is currently preparing to accept this responsibility within its area ... (*Proceedings ... Synodical Conference, 1961*, 24).

The completion of this incorporation brought the pilgrim journey into The Lutheran Church—Missouri Synod, which had been the major financial contributor to the Synodical Conference.

While no effort will be made to chart the course of development within the districts, it needs to be said that the Black Clergy Caucus emerged during this time and that a Centennial Committee for the 1977 observance was appointed. This Committee developed among other things the Centennial Celebration and prepared recommendations for the 1977 Convention at Dallas, Texas.

The Dallas Convention created the Commission on Black Ministry to do the following:

Plan, coordinate, and expand black ministry in the Synod in cooperation with the Convocation of Black Lutheran Congregations, the appropriate board chairman, and the President of the Synod.

Represent the concerns of black ministry before the boards, commissions, committees, and judicatories of the Synod (*Report*, 4-8).

This commission, with Dr. Richard Dickinson as executive director, provided inspiration, information, and motivation for the pilgrim journey in The Lutheran Church—Missouri Synod. As a pilgrim on and leader for the journey, Dr. Dickinson gave his full energy to this ministry. First among his contribution is clarifying the way for black ministry and placing emphasis on it, then developing models for black ministry in districts, and initiating of recognition for black ministry workers. The 1990 Black Ministry Task Force Report provided a summary of the Commission work under his leadership.

> The Task Force Report identified 108 programmatic activities by the Commission on Black Ministry from 1978-89. The scope of the activities includes planning, coordinating, and expanding black ministry in the LCMS. The 108 activities were listed. The report states, "Many of these activities have successful conclusion, some have not yet been resolved, and some are ongoing, as is black ministry in the LCMS" (*Report*, 18-19).

During this period of time, convocations developed by the Commission on Black Ministry linked congregations, members, teachers, and pastors together as pilgrims on the journey in the Lutheran church. "Lord, I want Jesus to walk with me all along this pilgrim journey" is among the many spirituals used in the worship experiences. Through these convocations, African Americans have come to own the ministry and to assume the leadership for it.

According to the Task Force Report, the significance of the convocations is that "each convocation strengthened the one before it and advanced black ministry." The Task Force report offered the convocation synopsis as follows:

1978   The Selma Convocation hosted the first black youth gathering and adopted resolutions that set the directions for the Commission.

1980   The Chicago Convocation reaffirmed the Selma resolutions and resolved to become self-supporting.

1982   The New York Convocation and Youth Gathering, held prior to the convocation, addressed the Task Force II recommendation to discontinue the Commission at the 1986 Synodical Convention. The response was, "Leave the Commission alone."

1983   The black district idea emerged due to problems on LCMS college campuses and other concerns. This idea was seen as people having greater impact and power over their own destiny.

1984   The St. Louis Family Convocation was credited with saving the Commission. The Convocation recommended that the president of the Synod convene a summit conference consisting of Synod and district leaders in black ministry. This convocation was self-supporting.

1986   The Indianapolis Convocation reaffirmed the 1984 resolution to the Synod to "leave the commission alone."

1988   The Memphis Family Convocation emerged with fellowship as the dominant theme. It resolved to move to an annual convocation.

1989   The Wichita Convocation put into place the mechanism for replacement at the retirement of the executive director, effective March 31, 1990. Again, a task force was convened to study black ministry and to make its recommendation to the president of the Synod by January 1, 1991.

1990   The Charlotte Convocation, with some youth in attendance, had worship as a dominant emphasis. The executive leadership of the Commission passed from Dr. Richard Dickinson to Dr. Bryant E. Clancy, Jr. This convocation reestablished connection with Africa and invited Dr. Nelson Unwene to be the keynote speaker for the 1991 Convocation.

1991   The Concordia College, Selma, Convocation hosted Dr. and Mrs. Nelson Unwene; received the report of their tour of black ministry congregations in the U. S. and established scholarships in their honor; rejoiced in the progress of Concordia College moving toward becoming a four-year institution; and set the stage with greater emphases on reaching new people with the Gospel.

1992 The Pittsburgh Convocation featured William Gray III, President and Chief Executive Officer, United Negro College Fund, as the keynote speaker; installed Dr. Philip Campbell as Director of Mission Networking; was inspired by Spirit-filled worship services and gospel singing; established annual convocations; and expressed concern over the organizational structure of the Synod as it related to black ministry (*Report,* 19–23).

SHAPING THE FUTURE OF BLACK MINISTRY IN THE LUTHERAN CHURCH

The Charlotte Convocation in 1990 provided the bridge to the future. The thorough study of black ministry as authorized by the Wichita Convention was in process, and delegates had the opportunity to offer ideas and proposals. The mantle of leadership was passed to a new executive director. Our need and dependence on our Lord Jesus to walk with us on the pilgrim journey was the signal through the full worship services at the beginning and ending of each day and the enthusiastic acceptance of it. The resolution to reach out to our sisters and brothers in Africa was embraced and claimed as an expense of the convocation. The leadership was changing with neither bitterness nor rancor but with a strong desire to get on with this work the Lord had given us to do in the dawning of a new decade, a decade that would end in a new century.

The Task Force issued the report and recommendations to the president of the Synod on January 9, 1991. With the support and encouragement of the president, the report was sent to every leader in the Synod through the office in which one served. The report contained a 20-year look at baptized members and contributions. A graph of the membership finding indicated a high of 140,000 in 1970 and a low of 80,000 in 1988, which was presented as being a 50,000 loss.

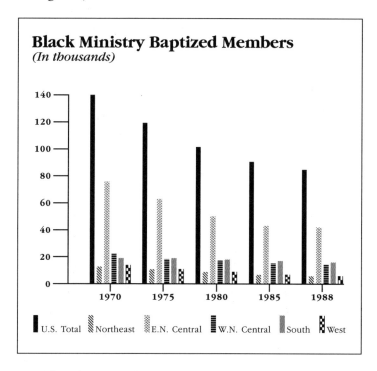

The above graph makes reaching new people central in the future of black ministry.

The Task Force report stated that the membership graph at first glance drew attention to the dramatic decline which then sloped off, suggesting that timely action can change the course of it. While the decline and slope of it in the different regions of the country varies, the end result is the same: timely action by synodical and black leadership can change the course of it.

In the mid-1970s, membership appeared to be affected by the St. Louis Seminary controversy. It caused some black congregations, leaders, and members to leave the Synod. The desegregation of American society contributed, in that no new congregations were initiated. Energy that should have been expended in mission development (cf. the Great Commission) had to be diverted to integrating the church and structure at every level.

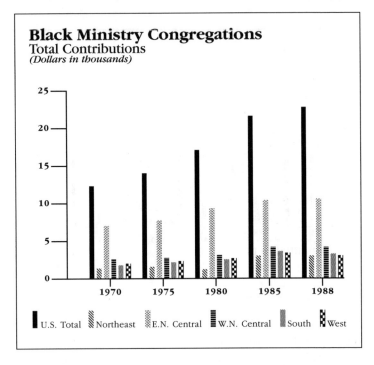

Black Ministry Congregations
Total Contributions
(Dollars in thousands)

The above graph showing the contributions of members is as dramatic in incline as the membership graph is in decline. The report of the Task Force stated, "It is clear that black people are contributing to the mission and ministry in the LCMS, black people stand as partners in mission and ministry, and black people can be counted on to do those timely things which will reverse the downward trend in membership and continue the upward direction in contributions" (*Report,* 27–28).This is part of the agenda of the future.

TheTask Force Report projected a vision for black ministry for the decade of the 90s and the new century. In that visionary statement this chapter is mirrored.

> Moved by the faith that our gracious and merciful God is incarnate in our Lord Jesus Christ, that the Holy Spirit calls us into and keeps us in "the one true faith," encouraged by the promises of God to be with us, the Task Force envisions a future for black ministry that is

> intentionally reaching out to all people

> excited about the scripture and being Lutheran

> people-oriented

> free to serve, to witness, to fellowship, to celebrate, to take initiative in congregations, to do ministry in districts, in the synod and everywhere as God wills.

> committed to preaching, teaching, and administering the Holy Sacraments, according to the Word of God so that God will be glorified and the people of God in congregations, in districts, in the synod and everywhere will serve God and one another with glad and good hearts, through faith in our Lord Jesus Christ.

> 1. The vision is that blacks are in decision-making positions for black ministry at all levels of the church.

> 2. The vision is that black Lutheran congregations in black communities are what the black church has been historically, namely, social, educational, political, nurturing; bolster of self-esteem, dignity, and humanity;

and pivotal to life and well-being of the total community (a bearer of the burdens of the community), etc.

3. The vision is that the administration of black ministry
is unified under the roof of the Commission on Black
Ministry so that those in black ministry can focus on the
total needs of black ministry in the church.

4. The vision is that the Commission on Black Ministry
has the authority to determine needs, coordinate solutions, and to network resources to meet the needs for
the sake of the Gospel.

5. The vision is that black ministry through the
Commission on Black Ministry, in keeping with the
Handbook, is worldwide in scope.

6. The vision is that the Commission on Black Ministry
implements ongoing strategic planning to address present and future needs.

7. The vision is that black membership in the LCMS is
doubled by the year 2000 (*Report,* 27-28).

The transfer of the position of Counselor for Black
Ministry from the Board for Mission Services to the
Commission on Black Ministry is the first step toward making a vision a reality. Creating the position of Mission
Networking and calling Dr. Philip Campbell to serve as
director is a critical factor in making the vision more than
a paper report. In the space of two years, 14 congregations
have, by the grace of God, been networked into being. The
broad acceptance of Dr. Campbell's work and the willing-
ness of district and synodical leaders to partner with his
office for the sake of new mission fields have newly
inspired a dream whose time has come. It is a clear signal
from God that He is with this ministry. The future is unfold-
ing in ways that touch those deep yearnings of African

Americans to give leadership to this ministry and to the work of the Lutheran church.

As this chapter is written, Mrs. Beverly McCray is being added to the Staff of the Commission on Black Ministry as Director, Family Life and Education Resources. This will enable congregations to network with one another to continue and increase the effects they have had historically in their communities.

We will strengthen our ties to Nigeria and Ghana, West Africa, as Dr. Paul Fynn, President of the Lutheran Church, Ghana, serves as keynote speaker at the 1994 Convocation. This, too, is part of the vision for black ministry, and it is becoming a reality.

The structure sketch for black ministry now and into the future is explained in the flow chart below.

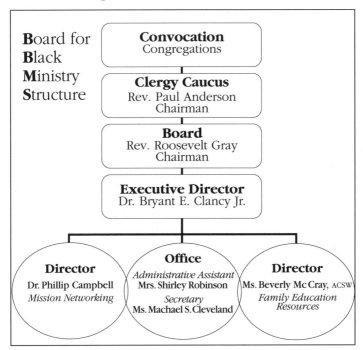

Board for Black Ministry Structure

Convocation
Congregations

Clergy Caucus
Rev. Paul Anderson
Chairman

Board
Rev. Roosevelt Gray
Chairman

Executive Director
Dr. Bryant E. Clancy Jr.

Director
Dr. Phillip Campbell
Mission Networking

Office
Administrative Assistant
Mrs. Shirley Robinson
Secretary
Ms. Machael S. Cleveland

Director
Ms. Beverly Mc Cray, ACSW
Family Education Resources

In this sketch the flow of information, direction, and activity is up to the Convocation and down from the Convocation to the staff. Congregations in black ministry send delegates and members to the annual convocations. The Clergy Caucus is central to the work of the convocation. It meets prior to the Convocation, thereby providing opportunity for the Commission to receive wise counsel, critique of reports, and support for intended action. The downward flow of information from the Convocation is through the Clergy Caucus as well.

Through this understanding of ministry organization, black ministry is positioned to respond to the new structure in The Lutheran Church—Missouri Synod. We can sit at the decision-making table as partner and fellow worker for Christ. We can advocate with boards and the university system, the Council of Administrators, the Conference of Congregational services, and the districts in order to increase the number of African American Lutherans from 50,000 to 100,000 by the new century.

In 1990, the Commission on Black Ministry prepared this Mission Statement, target, and goals:

> Being empowered by God, called to carry out the Great Commission, undergirded by the Black Ministry Convocation, the mission of the Commission on Black Ministry is to:
>
> Garner attention, resources, energy, knowledge, and the diverse gifts God has given His people to advocate change, nourish, affirm, encourage members in the faith, and reach new peoples with the Gospel all over the world.
>
> Goals of the Commission
>
> 1. Target: Link to black leaders

Create a vehicle that supports the unity of all ministries among blacks.

2. Target: Recruitment
Recruit black professional church workers, and devise ways in which to support them financially.

3. Target: Worldwide relationships
Establish a strong relationship with our sisters and brothers worldwide.

4. Target: Lay ministry training
Develop an improved and more comprehensive lay ministry training program in black ministry.

5. Target: Styles of ministry
Affirm and develop different styles of ministry and worship.

6. Target: Talent/resource bank
Develop a talent/resource bank to be of service to individuals, congregations, districts, and the Synod.

7. Target: Concordia College, Selma, Alabama
Continue strong support for Concordia College, Selma, Alabama.

8. Target: Funding agencies
Identify and utilize various funding agencies, private and governmental, to increase the ministry of our Lord.

9. Target: District networking
Expand the networking of district leaders and district involvement in black ministry.

10. Target: Black ministry agenda
Implement the issues of the *Black Ministry Agenda*

11. Target: Elementary and secondary education
Continue strong support for elementary and secondary education in urban centers.

Having a vision and goals in place and a structure to achieve them, energized by people with eyes on the promises of God and with the faith that God is with us, that "Jesus is walking with us all along this pilgrim journey," the Commission is nurturing members in the faith and reaching new people with the Gospel.

The approach involves a three-step process. 1) Encouraging 30 congregations to reach for their potential as mega-churches. 2) Planting and nurturing new mission fields at the rate of four to six a year. 3) Urging all remaining congregations to step to the next higher level of ministry. In all three steps members are nurtured in the faith and new people are claimed for the kingdom of God.

The future is one of hard work. This is what the past has been. It is what we see in the present. The hard work of reaching people for Christ is universal. St. Paul is talking about hard work in 2 Corinthians 4:8-11 NIV:

> We are hard pressed on every side, but not crushed; perplexed, but not in despair; persecuted, but not abandoned; struck down, but not destroyed. We always carry around in our body the death of Jesus, so that the life of Jesus may also be revealed in our body. For we who are alive are always being given over to death for Jesus' sake, so that his life may be revealed in our mortal body.

It is because of this hard work that we sing,

> *I want Jesus to walk with me;*
> *I want Jesus to walk with me;*
> *All along my pilgrim journey,*
> *Lord, I want Jesus to walk with me.*

May God make good to this ministry His promise, "Surely I am with you always, to the very end of the age" (Matthew 28:20 NIV).

Bibliography

Dickinson, Richard C. *Roses and Thorns.* St. Louis: Concordia Publishing House, 1977.

Johnson, Jeff G. *Black Christians: The Untold Lutheran Story.* St. Louis: Concordia Publishing House, 1991.

Mueller, John Theodore. *Diamond Jubilee, Evangelical Lutheran Synodical Conference of North America, 1872-1947.* St. Louis: Concordia Publishing House, 1948.

Proceedings of the Recessed Forty-Sixth Convention of the Lutheran Synodical Conference, May 17-19, 1961. St. Louis: Concordia Publishing House, 1961.

Report of Task Force on Black Ministry in the Lutheran Church—Missouri Synod. St. Louis: The Lutheran Church—Missouri Synod, 1991.

Synodical Conference Proceedings, vol. 33-39. St. Louis: Concordia Publishing House, 1932.

Synodical Conference Proceedings, vol. 43-46. St. Louis: Concordia Publishing House, 1954.

Young, Rosa. *Light in the Dark Belt.* Rev. ed. St. Louis: Concordia Publishing House, 1950.

SUGGESTED VIDEOS

Called Out and Sent Back. St. Louis: The Lutheran Church-Missouri Synod, 1987.

His Word ... Our Language. St. Louis: The Lutheran Church—Missouri Synod, 1988.

The Key to Our Mission: Concordia College, Selma. St. Louis: The Lutheran Church—Missouri Synod, 1990.

The Right Tool. St. Louis: The Lutheran Church—Missouri Synod, 1988.

Favorite Negro Spirituals

It's Me

Refrain
It's me, it's me, O Lord,
Standing in the need of prayer;
It's me, it's me, O Lord,
Standing in the need of prayer.

Stanzas

Not my brother, but it's me, O Lord,
Standing in the need of prayer;
Not my brother, but it's me, O Lord,
Standing in the need of prayer.

Not my sister, but it's me, O Lord,
Standing in the need of prayer;
Not my sister, but it's me, O Lord,
Standing in the need of prayer.

Not my mother, but it's me, O Lord,
Standing in the need of prayer;
Not my mother, but it's me, O Lord,
Standing in the need of prayer.

Not my elder, but it's me, O Lord,
Standing in the need of prayer;
Not my elder, but it's me, O Lord,
Standing in the need of prayer.

Joshua Fit de Battle of Jericho

Refrain
Joshua fit de battle of Jericho,
Jericho, Jericho,
Joshua fit de battle of Jericho,
An' de walls come tumblin' down.

Stanzas
You may talk about yo' king ob Gideon;
You may talk about yo' man ob Saul;
Dere's none like good ole Joshua
Af de battle of Jericho.

Up to de walls ob Jericho
He marched with spear in han'.
"Go blow dem ram horns," Joshua cried,
"Kase de battle am in my han'."

Den de lam ram sheep horns begin to blow;
Trumpets begin to sound.
Joshua commanded de chillen to shout,
An' de walls come bumblin' down.

Kum Ba Yah

Refrain
Kum ba yah, my Lord, Kum ba yah!
Kum ba yah, my Lord, Kum ba yah!
Kum ba yah, my Lord, Kum ba yah!
O Lord, Kum ba yah.

Stanzas
Someone's crying, Lord, Kum ba yah …

Someone's singing, Lord, Kum ba yah …

Someone's praying, Lord, Kum ba yah …

(And so on. It could end with "Come by here,
Lord, Kum ba yah …").

Lord, I Want to Be a Christian

Refrain
In a my heart, in a my heart,
Lord, I want to be a Christian in a my heart.

Stanzas
Lord, I want to be a Christian
in a my heart, in a my heart,
Lord, I want to be a Christian in a my heart.

Lord, I want to be more loving
in a my heart, in a my heart,
Lord, I want to be more loving in a my heart.

Lord, I want to be more holy
in a my heart, in a my heart,
Lord, I want to be more holy in a my heart.

I don't want to be like Judas
in a my heart, in a my heart,
I don't want to be like Judas in a my heart.

Lord, I want to be like Jesus
in a my heart, in a my heart,
Lord, I want to be like Jesus in a my heart.

My Lord, What a Mourning

Refrain
My Lord, what a mourning,
My Lord, what a mourning,
My Lord, what a mourning,
When the stars begin to fall.

Stanzas
You'll hear the trumpet sound
To wake the nations underground,
Looking to my God's right hand,

When the stars begin to fall.

You'll hear the sinner mourn,
To wake the nations underground,
Looking to my God's right hand,
When the stars begin to fall.

You'll hear the Christian shout,
To wake the nations underground,
Looking to my God's right hand,
When the stars begin to fall.

Nobody Knows the Trouble I've Seen

Refrain
Oh, nobody knows the trouble I've seen,
Nobody knows but Jesus!
Nobody knows the trouble I've seen,
Glory Hallelujah!

Stanzas
Sometimes I'm up, sometimes I'm down;
Oh yes, Lord;
Sometimes I'm almost to the ground,
Oh yes, Lord.
Although you see me going along so,
Oh yes, Lord;
I have my trials here below, Oh yes, Lord.

One day when I was walking along,
Oh yes, Lord,
The element open'd, and the Love came down,
Oh yes, Lord.
I never shall forget that day,
Oh yes, Lord,
When Jesus wash'd my sins away,
Oh yes, Lord.

O Mary, Don't You Weep

Refrain
O Mary, don't you weep, don't you mourn,
O Mary, don't you weep, don't you mourn;
Pharaoh's army got drownded, O Mary, don't
   you weep.

Stanzas
Some of these mournings bright and fair,
Take my wings and cleave the air,
Pharaoh's army got drownded, O Mary, don't
   you weep.

When I get to heaven goin' to sing and shout,
Nobody there for to turn me out,
Pharaoh's army got drowned, O Mary, don't you
   weep.

Somebody's Knocking at Your Door

Refrain
Somebody's knocking at your door,
Somebody's knocking at your door;
O sinner, why don't you answer?
Somebody's knocking at your door.

Stanzas
Knocks like Jesus,
Somebody's knocking at your door;
Knocks like Jesus,
Somebody's knocking at your door.

Can't you hear Him?
Somebody's knocking at your door;
Can't you hear Him?
Somebody's knocking at your door.

Answer Jesus,
Somebody's knocking at your door;
Answer Jesus,
Somebody's knocking at your door.

Jesus calls you,
Somebody's knocking at your door;
Jesus calls you,
Somebody's knocking at your door.

Can't you trust Him?
Somebody's knocking at your door;
Can't you trust Him?
Somebody's knocking at your door.

Steal Away

Refrain
Steal away, steal away,
steal away to Jesus!
Steal away, steal away home,
I ain't got long to stay here!

Stanzas
My Lord calls me,
He calls me by the thunder,
The trumpet sounds within my soul,
I ain't got long to stay here.

Green trees are bending,
poor sinner stands a trembling,
The trumpet sounds within my soul,
I ain't got long to stay here.

Tombstones are bursting,
poor sinner stands a trembling,
The trumpet sounds within my soul,
I ain't got long to stay here.

My Lord calls me,
He calls me by the lightning,
The trumpet sounds within my soul,
I ain't got long to stay here.

Swing Low

Refrain
Swing low, sweet chariot,
Coming for to carry me home,
Swing low, sweet chariot,
Coming for to carry me home.

Stanzas
I looked over Jordan, and what did I see?
Coming for to carry me home,
A band of angels coming after me,
Coming for to carry me home.

If you get there before I do,
Coming for to carry me home,
Tell all my friends I'm coming, too,
Coming for to carry me home.

I'm sometimes up, I'm sometimes down,
Coming for to carry me home,
But still my soul feels heav'nly bound,
Coming for to carry me home.

We Shall Overcome

Stanzas
We shall overcome,
We shall overcome,
We shall overcome some day.
Oh, deep in my heart, I do believe,
We shall overcome someday.

The Lord will see us through,
The Lord will see us through,
The Lord will see us through someday.
Oh, deep in my heart, I do believe,
The Lord will see us through someday.

We're on to victory,
We're on to victory,

We're on to victory someday.
Oh, deep in my heart, I do believe,
We're on to victory someday.

We'll walk hand in hand,
We'll walk hand in hand,
We'll walk hand in hand, someday.
Oh, deep in my heart, I do believe,
We'll walk hand in hand someday.

We are not afraid,
We are not afraid,
We are not afraid today.
Oh, deep in my heart, I do believe,
We are not afraid today.

The truth shall make us free,
The truth shall make us free,
The truth shall make us free someday.
Oh, deep in my heart, I do believe,
The truth shall make us free someday.

We shall live in peace,
We shall live in peace,
We shall live in peace someday.
Oh, deep in my heart, I do believe,
We shall live in peace someday.

Were You There

Were you there when they crucified my Lord?
Were you there when they crucified my Lord?
Oh, sometimes it causes me to tremble, tremble,
    tremble.
Were you there when they crucified my Lord?

Were you there when they nailed him to the tree?
Were you there when they nailed him to the tree?
Oh, sometimes it causes me to tremble, tremble,
    tremble.
Were you there when they nailed him to the tree?

Were you there when they laid him in the tomb?
Were you there when they laid him in the tomb?
Oh, sometimes it causes me to tremble, tremble,
tremble.
Were you there when they laid him in the tomb?

Were you there when he rose up from the dead?
Were you there when he rose up from the dead?
Oh, sometimes it causes me to tremble, tremble,
tremble.
Were you there when he rose up from the dead?

Bibliography

Beattie, John W., et al, eds. *The Gray Book of Favorite Songs.* Chicago: Hall & McCreary Company, 1924.

Benziger, Barbara, and Eleanor Dickinson. *That Old-Time Religion, One Hundred Hymns, Songs, and Stories.* New York: Harper & Row, 1975.

Steyer, Martin W., ed. *Hymns for Now II.* St. Louis: Concordia Publishing House, 1969.

Walker, Wyatt Tee. *Somebody's Calling My Name: Black Sacred Music and Social Change.* Valley Forge: Judson Press, 1985.

Some Pioneers of Lutheranism among Blacks

Black Clergy Caucus
A unit of the
Commission on Black
Ministry of The
Lutheran Church—
Missouri Synod.

Christ Lutheran Church
Rosebud, Alabama (1946).
Founded in 1916 as the first
Lutheran church among
Alabama blacks.

Marmaduke N. Carter
Served with Rosa J. Young
in Alabama mission work.
Lectured in Midwest con-
gregations to promote mis-
sion support for Alabama.
Founder of St. Philip
Congregation, Chicago, IL.

Albert Dominick
Served Trinity, Selma, and
Saint Timothy, East Selma.
Secretary of Alabama
Lutheran Conference.
Instructor at Alabama
Lutheran Academy, Selma.

Peter R. Hunt
Served several Alabama
rural congregations. Dean
of students, professor, and
president pro tem,
Concordia College, Selma.

R. F. Jenkins
Pastor of Alabama rural congregations. Served congregations in Charlotte, N.C.,
and Omaha, Nebraska.
Instructor at Alabama
Lutheran Academy, Selma.

Joseph Lavalais
Pastor of St. Philip Lutheran
Church, Philadelphia.
Chairman of Philadelphia
Pastoral Conference. Vice
president of The Lutheran
Church—Missouri Synod.

Chineta Lawhorn
Teacher and missionary in
Alabama schools. Matron at
Alabama Lutheran Academy,
Selma.

Harvey Lehman
Served Christ Church,
Rosebud. Pastor of Rosa J.
Young. Also served congre-
gations in Buffalo, N.Y., and
Los Angeles, CA. Chaplain
at Morningside Hospital,
Los Angeles, CA.

R. O. L. Lynn
First president of Concordia
College, Alabama. Dean of
Immanuel College and
Seminary, Greensboro, N.C.

Rosa J. Young
Founder of Lutheranism
among blacks in Alabama.
Teacher at Rosebud and
Matron at Alabama Lutheran
Academy, Selma.

APPENDIX C
Clergy Roster (as of November 1995)

Rev. Paul Anderson
Holy Cross Lutheran Church
500 E. Mount Pleasant Avenue
Philadelphia, PA 19119

Rev. Donald Anthony
5408 Gardenwood Road
Baltimore, MD 21206

Rev. Russell Belisle
St. Philip Lutheran Church
6232 S. Eberhart Avenue
Chicago, IL 60637

Rev. Victor Belton
Peace Lutheran Church
1679 Columbia Drive
Decatur, GA 30032

Rev. Arthur Bodley
9640 S. LaSalle Street
Chicago, IL 60628

Rev. Christopher Bodley
Our Savior Lutheran Church
1750 Bruton Boulevard
Orlando, FL 32805

Dr. Simon Bodley
5624 Bartmer Street
St. Louis, MO 63112

Rev. John Brazeal
1405 S. 12th Avenue
Maywood, IL 60153

Rev. James Brown
8595 Untreiner Avenue
Pensacola, FL 32514

Rev. Johnny Brown
#4 Brown Street
Camden, AL 32504

Dr. Phillip Campbell
1206 Meramec Heights
Manchester, MO 63021

Rev. Lynell Carter
412-31 N. Broadway
Yonkers, NY 10701

Rev. Michael Carter
1129 N. Jackson Street, #607-C
Milwaukee, WI 53202

Dr. Bryant Clancy
643 Highland Glen Drive
Ballwin, MO 63021

Rev. Moses Clark
P. O. Box 369
Atmore, AL 36502

Rev. Gerald Coleman
Fountain of Life Lutheran Church
328 Hopkins Road
Kernersville, NC 27284

Rev. Robert Collins
17000 Greenwood Avenue
South Holland, IL 60473

Lt. Col. Samuel Cosby
27 CSG/HC
Cannon AFB, NM 88103

Rev. John H. Davis
P. O. Box 416
Camden, AL 36726

Rev. Warren Davis
7041 Kelvin Terrace
Pensacola, FL 32503

Rev. Kevin Dean
7936 S. Eberhart #1
Chicago, IL 60619

Rev. David DeRamus
Concordia College
1804 Green Street
Selma, AL 36701

Dr. Marshall Dennis
Pilgrim Lutheran Church
447 N. First Street
Birmingham, AL 35205

Dr. Richard C. Dickinson
4325 Delmar Boulevard
St. Louis, MO 63108

Rev. Homer Diggs
6429 N. 73d Street
Milwaukee, WI 53208

Dr. Albert Dominick
7073 Caprice Drive
Baton Rouge, LA 70812

Rev. Venice Douglas
13030 Mackenzie Street
Detroit, MI 48228

Rev. Percy Dumas
2372 Tennessee Street
Gary, IN 46407

Rev. James Eddleman
125 Pistachio
Dumas, AR 71639

Rev. Rodney Emilien
Grace Lutheran Church
1066 Washington Avenue
Montgomery, AL 38104

Rev. Steve Everette
Zion Lutheran Church
1924 St. Charles Avenue
New Orleans, LA 70130

Dr. Howard Foard
7412 S. Michigan Street
Chicago, IL 60619

Rev. Larry Frazier
Resurrection Lutheran Church
9349 S. Wentworth Avenue
Chicago, IL 60620

Rev. Lloyd Gaines
Mt. Olivet Lutheran Church
1306-08 Vermont Avenue NW
Washington, DC 20005

Rev. Duane Geary
Messiah Lutheran Church
630 E. Front Street
Plainfield, NJ 07060

Rev. C. R. Gerhold
R. D. #3, Box 2475
Honesdale, PA 18431

Rev. Rozell Gilmore
3909 N. Overlook Terrace
Portland, OR 97227

Rev. Hanes Glaspie
Mt. Olive Lutheran Church
1828 Barrett Avenue
Richmond, CA 94801

Rev. Juan Gonzalez
Our Savior Lutheran Church
2362 NW 95th Street
Miami, FL 33147

African Americans and the Local Church

Rev. Roosevelt Gray
Concordia Theological Seminary
6600 N. Clinton Street
Fort Wayne, IN 46825

Rev. Timothy Green
Redeemer Lutheran Church
116-01 204th Street
St. Albans, NY 11412

Rev. William Griffen
16050 Lake Shore Road
Union Pier, MI 49129

Rev. Mark Griffin
St. Philip Lutheran Church
1230 Isiah Montgomery Street
Jackson, MS 39203

Rev. Marvin Griffin
7681 Wave Drive
New Orleans, LA 70128

Rev. George Gunter
2881A Casey Street
San Diego, CA 92139

Rev. Byrene K. Haney
7047 Tireman
Detroit, MI 48204

Rev. Herman Hawkins
5154 N. Marty #106
Fresno, CA 93711

Rev. Samuel Henderson
St. Philip Lutheran Church
2884 E. Grand Boulevard
Detroit, MI 48202

Dr. Edgar Holmes
5327 W. Columbia Avenue
Philadelphia, PA 19131

Rev. Samuel Hoard
P. O. Box 550830
Orlando, FL 32855

Rev. Harold James
2351 Crestwood Circle
Mobile, AL 36617

Dr. Julius Jenkins
Concordia College
1804 Green Street
Selma, AL 36617

Rev. R. F. Jenkins
3110 Lincoln Boulevard
Omaha, NE 68132

Dr. Jeff Johnson
4194 Leimert Boulevard #1
Los Angeles, CA 90008

Rev. John Johnson
Mount Calvary Lutheran Church
P. O. Box 250
Kannapolis, NC 28082

Rev. Channing Kearney
% Immanuel Lutheran Church
P. O. Box 552
New Plymouth, ID 83655

Dr. Robert King
901 Roland Court
Jefferson City, MO 65101

Rev. Gulfrey Laurent
19316 Northwood Avenue
Carson, CA 90746

Rev. Glenn Lucas
St. Paul Lutheran Church
1309 W. Adams Boulevard
Los Angeles, CA 90018

Rev. Willie Lucas
Unity Lutheran Church
4200 Caseyville Avenue
East St. Louis, IL 62204

Rev. Robert Malone
St. John Lutheran Church
4545 Benton Street
Kansas City, MO 64230

Rev. Prentice Marsh
Ephphatha Lutheran Church
7956 Martin Luther King Drive
Chicago, IL 60619

Rev. William Marsh
Route 1, Box 6L
Pine Hill, AL 36769

Rev. Frank Marshall
St. Paul Lutheran Church
2730 W. Edgewood Avenue
Jacksonville, FL 32209

Rev. James B. Marshall
306 Laurdes Circle East
Mobile, AL 36617

Rev. Ulmer Marshall
6405 St. Thomas Court
Mobile, AL 36618

Rev. Elder McCants
Community Lutheran Church
5063 Rigsby Street
San Antonio, TX 78222

Rev. Jimmy McCants
Trinity Lutheran Church
5234 N. Clairborne Avenue
New Orleans, LA 70130

Rev. Reholma McCants
Unity Lutheran Church
7825½ Hamilton
Pittsburgh, PA 15208

Rev. James McDaniels
Grace Lutheran Church
1315 E. Washington Street
Greensboro, NC 27401

Rev. Louis Miller
1253 Thomas SE
Grand Rapids, MI 49506

Rev. John Nunes
Historic Trinity Lutheran Church
1345 Gratiot Avenue
Detroit, MI 48207

Dr. Frazier Odom
1640 Grape Street
St. Louis, MO 63147

Rev. William Parson
3420 Cumberland Road
Winston-Salem, NC 27105

Rev. John Plump
311 N. Beach Boulevard
Anaheim, CA 42801

Rev. John Poole
359 Cozart Court
Concord, NC 28025

Rev. Quentin Poulson
Resurrection Lutheran Church
2500 Seminary Avenue
Richmond, VA 23220

Dr. McNair Ramsey
Concordia College
1804 Green Street
Selma, AL 36701

Rev. Kermit Ratcliffe
Concordia University
12800 N. Lake Shore Drive
Mequon, WI 53092

Rev. Carl Robinson
Good Shepherd Lutheran Church
P. O. Box 22639
Seattle, WA 98122

Rev. Richard Robinson
St. Paul Lutheran Church
5707 S. Marsalis Avenue
Dallas, TX 75241

Rev. Timothy Seals
Hope Memorial Lutheran Church
3401 Somerset
Los Angeles, CA 90018

Chaplain Douglas Shamburger
Marine Corp Base
Cape LeJeuine, NC 28542

Rev. Marcus Sims
240 S. 57th Street
Philadelphia, PA 19139

Rev. John Skinner
4402 Saint Anthony
New Orleans, LA 70122

Rev. Benjamin Stallworth
% Ms. Dorothy Mitchell
P. O. Box 20
Fairhope, AL 36533

Rev. Deric Taylor
St. Peter Lutheran Church
105 Highland Place
Brooklyn, NY 11208

Rev. Edwin Thompson
P. O. Box 107
Killona, LA 70066

Rev. Othneil Thompson
6629 Quincy Street
Philadelphia, PA 19119

Rev. James Tyler
3104 Vassar Street
Bakersfield, CA 93306

Rev. Steve Washington
Trinity Lutheran Church
1900 Range Street
Selma, AL 36701

Rev. Edward Watson
6274 Cates
University City, MO 63130

Rev. James Wiggins, Jr.
Outer Drive Faith Lutheran
   Church
17500 James Couzens Highway
Detroit, MI 48235

Rev. James Wiggins, Sr.
Trinity Lutheran Church
1104 Rosa Parks Avenue
Montgomery, AL 36108

Rev. Steven Wiggins
Prince of Peace Lutheran Church
3001 Beatties Ford Road
Charlotte, NC 28216

Rev. Anthony Williams
14926 Avalon Street
Dolton, IL 60419

Rev. S. T. WIlliams, Jr.
Concordia Theological Seminary
6600 N. Clinton, Box 342
Fort Wayne, IN 46825

Rev. Jimmie Wilson
4348 Olive Street #106
St. Louis, MO 63108

APPENDIX C

Seminary Students (as of November 1995)

At Fort Wayne
Howard Alexander, colloquy program
Carl Brown, M.Div. program
Darrel Dennis, colloquy program
Charles Hines, M.Div. program
Elstner Lewis, colloquy program
Clarence Martin, colloquy program
Cecil Nixon, M.Div. program
Ibrahim Timbo, M.Div. program

At St. Louis
Wayne Lawrence, M.Div. program
Ronald Staples, special
James Turner, colloquy program
Michael Udoekong, M.Div. program
Alexander Whitfield, M.Div. program
Byron Williams, colloquy program